North Vietnamese peasants walk along a rice paddy dike.

WAR IN VIETNAM

BOOK I — Eve of Battle

By David K. Wright

CP CHILDRENS PRESS ®

CHICAGO

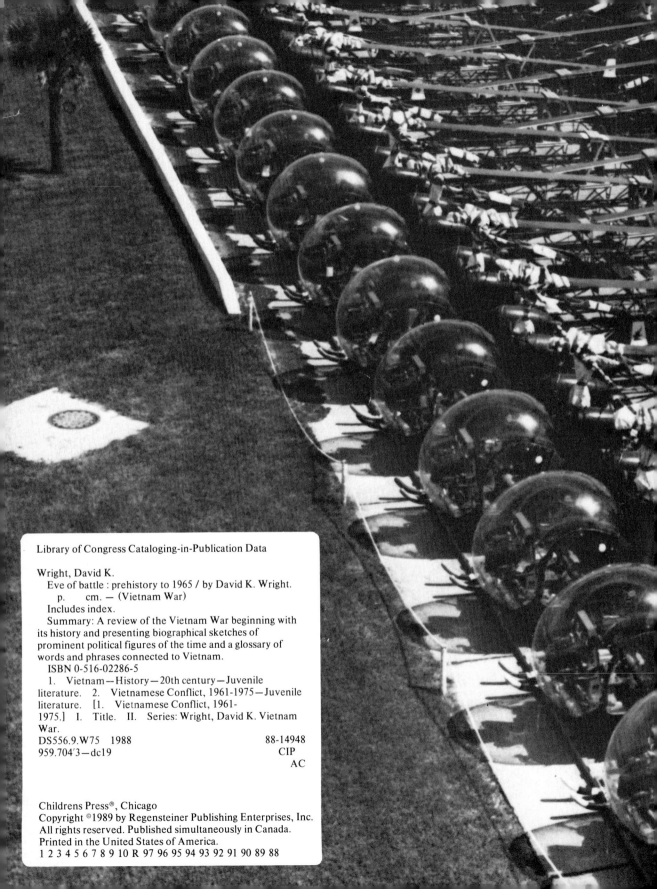

Library of Congress Cataloging-in-Publication Data

Wright, David K.
　Eve of battle : prehistory to 1965 / by David K. Wright.
　　p.　　cm. — (Vietnam War)
　Includes index.
　Summary: A review of the Vietnam War beginning with
its history and presenting biographical sketches of
prominent political figures of the time and a glossary of
words and phrases connected to Vietnam.
　ISBN 0-516-02286-5
　1.　Vietnam—History—20th century—Juvenile
literature.　2.　Vietnamese Conflict, 1961-1975—Juvenile
literature.　[1.　Vietnamese Conflict, 1961-
1975.]　I.　Title.　II.　Series: Wright, David K. Vietnam
War.
DS556.9.W75　1988　　　　　　　　　88-14948
959.704′3—dc19　　　　　　　　　　CIP
　　　　　　　　　　　　　　　　　　AC

Childrens Press®, Chicago
Copyright ©1989 by Regensteiner Publishing Enterprises, Inc.
All rights reserved. Published simultaneously in Canada.
Printed in the United States of America.
1 2 3 4 5 6 7 8 9 10 R 97 96 95 94 93 92 91 90 89 88

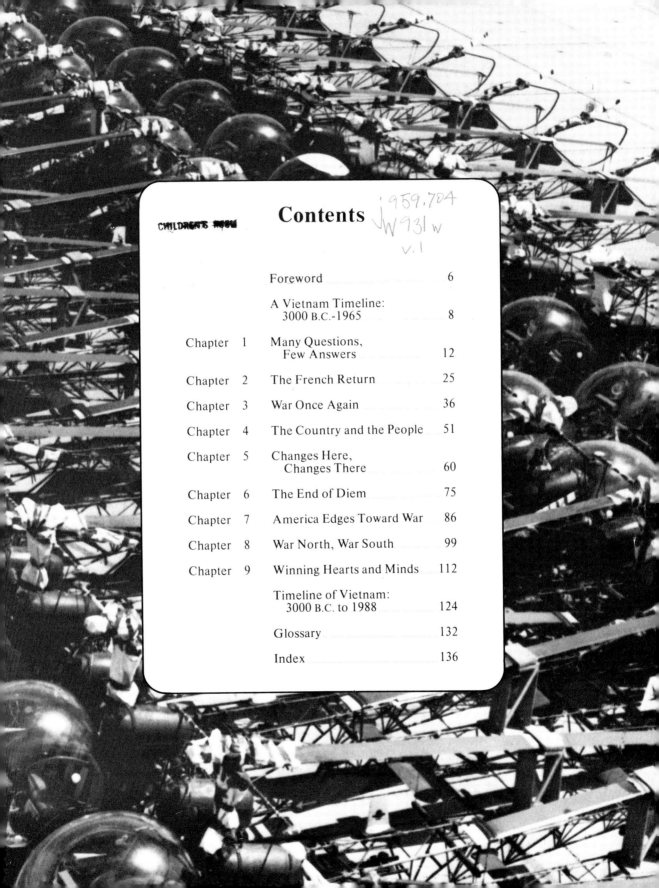

Contents

Foreword

Vietnam. The land, the war, the experience continue to haunt the nation. It was the first war America lost, and lost causes always seem to leave more questions than answers. The four-volume series *War in Vietnam* by David K. Wright looks at why the United States became involved, why we fought the war the way we did, and why we lost. In seeking answers to these questions, Mr. Wright contributes to the healing of the nation, which remains the unfinished business of the war.

In Book I — *Eve of Battle*, Wright describes the early history of Vietnam up to the critical year 1965, when the first U. S. combat troops arrived in South Vietnam. We learn of Vietnam's long tradition of fierce independence, the period of French rule over the country, the first French-Indochina war involving the nationalist Viet Minh, and the growing American involvement following the French defeat in 1954. Wright shows us how America's entanglement deepened step by step. By 1965 the leaders in Washington, D. C., felt they had no choice but to send U. S. combat troops to save Vietnam from communism. *Eve of Battle* reveals the danger of making important national decisions without really understanding the nature and history of the people we have pledged to support.

Book II — *A Wider War* explores one of the most puzzling questions of the conflict. Why couldn't the United States — the world's greatest military power — defeat a poorly equipped peasant army? Some argue that America's politicians would not use the military force necessary to win. But *A Wider War* shows that the amount of force Americans used was much greater than in any other war. Such firepower and violence — from the smallest infantry unit to the giant B-52 bombers — turned the Vietnamese peasants against the U. S. It turned many Americans against the war as well. To these people, including some Vietnam veterans, it appeared that time was on the enemy's side. Before long, many in America lost patience with this long, costly, and savage war.

Book III — *Vietnamization* tells of the events that followed the 1968 election of Richard Nixon as President. Even though Nixon had pledged to seek "peace with honor," he pursued a complex and at times dishonest policy in running the war. In violation of the law, Nixon ordered U.S. troops to invade Cambodia and Laos. We also learn how he promised to reduce the number of U. S. troops in Vietnam yet still increase support for the South Vietnamese Army. He stepped up the bombing of North Vietnam at the same time he began secret talks with the enemy in Paris. This book also wrestles with the agonizing question of how American soldiers could have taken part in the March 1968 massacre of innocent Vietnamese civilians. The My Lai 4 incident, in which hundreds of men, women, and children were murdered, remains a black mark against America's honor. The book concludes with the heavy Christmas bombing of North Vietnam in December 1972 and with the January 1973 cease-fire agreement. The treaty ended American involvement in Vietnam but did not end the war.

The final book — *The Fall of Vietnam* — recounts the tragic consequences of America's confused policies in Vietnam. In our efforts to bring democracy and freedom to this far-away nation, we nearly lost sight of these values at home. The Watergate political scandal showed that even President Nixon and his close advisors were willing to break the law to stay in power. Richard Nixon became the only President in history forced to resign in disgrace. In one sense he can be counted as a victim of Vietnam. More tragic victims were the populations of North and South Vietnam, Cambodia, and Laos. Many U. S. Vietnam veterans also remain troubled victims of the war. No one can predict when the agony will end for the families of MIAs — those reported missing in action from 1965 to 1973. These families have waited for years to hear some word about the fate of their loved ones.

Vietnam is a sad chapter in the nation's history. The series *War in Vietnam* will help readers find answers to many of their questions about the war. The biggest question of all may be — Was Vietnam an isolated, regrettable event, or did our conduct of the war reveal the darker side of the American character? The answer to this question, perhaps more than any other, has meaning for the nation's future.

Frank A. Burdick
Professor of History at
State University College
Cortland, New York

A Vietnam Timeline: Major Events in the Eve of Battle

3000 B.C.: The people we call the Vietnamese begin to migrate south out of China.

100 B.C.: Start of China's 1,000-year rule of Vietnam.

A.D. 938: Vietnam becomes independent.

1500: The first European explorers visit Vietnam.

1640: Alexandre de Rhodes, a French Roman Catholic missionary, arrives in Vietnam.

1744: Vietnam expands into the Mekong Delta. The Vietnamese by this date rule over all of present-day Vietnam.

1844: The French fleet destroys Vietnam's navy.

1859: Saigon falls to the French.

1883: The French capture Hanoi.

1930: Ho Chi Minh starts the Indochinese Communist Party.

1939: The communist party is outlawed in Vietnam.

A victim of fighting in Saigon, 1963.

1941:   The Japanese take control of Vietnam as Ho Chi Minh returns from a Chinese prison and the Viet Minh (communist army) is founded.

1945:   Ho Chi Minh declares Vietnam independent as the Japanese surrender.

1946:   The French return, and the Viet Minh take to the hills as the French Indochina war begins.

1952:   Viet Minh forces are defeated several times by the French.

1954:   The French are defeated at Dien Bien Phu and agree to leave Vietnam. Vietnam is divided into north and south following a cease-fire agreed upon in Geneva, Switzerland.

1955:   The U.S. begins to send aid to South Vietnam.

1956:   President Ngo Dinh Diem refuses to hold elections, as had been promised in the Geneva agreement.

March on Washington, D.C., 1963.

1957:   Communist guerrilla activities begin in South Vietnam.

1959:   The North Vietnamese start to send soldiers into South Vietnam.

1963:   The Viet Cong (South Vietnamese communists) defeat regular South Vietnamese soldiers at Ap Bac. This is the first major battle between the two sides. Buddhists protest South Vietnamese government policies. President Diem is overthrown and killed by the military.

1964:   A North Vietnamese patrol boat attacks an American destroyer in the Gulf of Tonkin. Congress gives President Lyndon B. Johnson special powers to act in Southeast Asia. The first American pilot is shot down and taken prisoner by the North Vietnamese.

1965:   American air raids take place over North Vietnam. The first American combat troops arrive in South Vietnam.

Helicopters prepare to land on a lonely road early in the war.

Chapter 1

Many Questions, Few Answers

Many years have passed since fighting stopped in Vietnam. The longest and most costly war in United States history left hundreds of thousands of people dead. Additional thousands in Southeast Asia remain homeless or without a country or without hope. You would think that everyone would have the same understanding of such a war, but this is not the case.

Scholars cannot even agree on exactly when the Vietnam War began or when it ended. Some believe it will not end until Vietnamese forces withdraw from neighboring Cambodia* and Laos or until all American prisoners of war are accounted for. Can the war be over if minorities inside Vietnam are still shooting at Vietnamese soldiers?

People learning about the Vietnam War usually have many questions. When did the war begin? When did the United States get involved and why? What was being a soldier like in Vietnam? What did it mean to "Bring the war home"? Why did the U.S. lose thousands of soldiers, then decide to withdraw? What was "Vietnamization"? Were we the "good guys" or the "bad guys"? Who won, or is the war still going on in Southeast Asia? What is Vietnam like today?

This series presents a brief history of Vietnam, then examines these and other questions from all sides. It isn't possible to talk to many of those who suffered most or to those who have since died. We must rely mainly on written records for information about early decisions and major battles. These records

* After the Vietnam War Cambodia was renamed Kampuchea. Since this series deals with events before 1975, the name Cambodia is used throughout.

U.S. Marines carry a wounded soldier through the rubble of Hué.

help us understand the history and terror of this strange war. Sadly, conflict has plagued Vietnam since its beginning.

The people we call Vietnamese are descended from natives of southern China who fled south about 3,000 B.C. They left to avoid being absorbed by the Chinese. The land where they settled borders the South China Sea, just above the equator in Southeast Asia. It is a long, narrow coastal plain backed by forbidding, jungle-covered mountains of little value for farming. In contrast, the Red River in the north and the Mekong River in the south created broad, fertile deltas ideal for growing rice. Modern Vietnam stretches 1,000 miles, from the border with China to the southern border of Cambodia. In central Vietnam, the country is only 50 miles wide.

Long before Europeans arrived in the sixteenth century, Vietnam's history was one of conflict. The early Vietnamese who settled the region first had to conquer the local people, such as those who lived in the kingdom of Champa along the central coast. As the Vietnamese slowly populated the south, they developed a unique language and a fierce determination to be independent. Few of them ventured into the central highlands, where the land was poor and where jungles concealed primitive tribespeople. Moving into the Mekong Delta far to the south, the Vietnamese pushed the native Cambodians westward and gained control of a wonderful rice-growing area.

Over the centuries, the Vietnamese continued to fight with their Chinese neighbors, with local minorities, and with each other. Eventually they were defeated by the Chinese and suffered under China's rule for more than 1,000 years. They learned a great deal from their rulers before staging a prolonged revolt that gained them independence in A.D. 938. The Vietnamese ruled themselves for nearly 600 years until the first Europeans arrived in the 1500s. For a time, the Vietnamese were able to turn back attempts by the Portugese, Dutch, British, and French troops to establish colonies.

A few Frenchmen, mostly Roman Catholic missionaries, remained in Vietnam to work

NAN CHAO
(CHINA)

Canton

TONKIN

LAN CHANG

LAO

ANNAM

Mekong River

SIAM

Angor

CHAMPA

CAMBODIA

Bay of
Bandon

(SOUTH
CHINA
SEA)

Kra
Isthmus

KRA

TAMBRALINGA

KEDAH

UJONG
TANAH

Brunei

(BORNEO)

MALAYU

SRIVIJAYA

BALI

HISTORICAL
MAP OF
SOUTHEAST ASIA

15TH Century A.D.

Singhasari

among the people. In 1647, missionary Alexandre de Rhodes adapted the Vietnamese language to the modern, Western alphabet. This increased French influence so much that by 1800 persecution of Christians by the dominant Buddhists and Confucians had stopped. A brief period of unity followed. Then, in 1857, the French invaded Vietnam in force. After a series of European victories, the country became a French colony in 1883.

The invasion took place for several reasons. The French saw other European powers taking over Asia and did not want to be left out of the region. Also, the industrial revolution meant that France needed raw materials and new countries to buy French goods. With modern gunboats and other weapons, they gradually overcame Vietnamese resistance. In fact, disease killed more Frenchmen during this period than did the poorly armed enemy.

The French split Vietnam into three countries and made all three part of the French Indochina Union. The union included neighboring Laos and Cambodia. Under French rule, a few Viet-

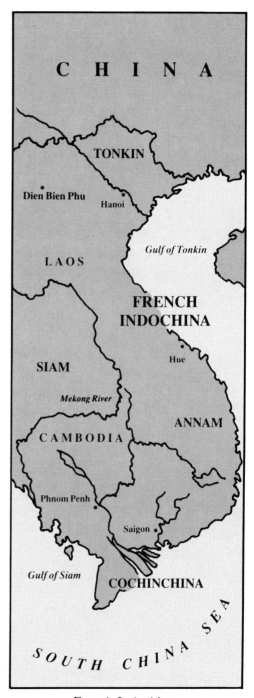

French Indochina.

namese received a modern, Catholic-influenced education and obtained jobs as politicians and managers.

Many Vietnamese, however, silently hated Western influence and Christianity. These were mainly small farmers or landless villagers who made a poor living working on European-owned rubber plantations, cultivating rice paddies, fishing, or running small shops. Their way of life has failed to improve even in the twentieth century.

It's easy from a modern viewpoint to be critical of the French invasion and rule of Indochina. At the time, however, most of the French felt they were bringing civilization and the one true religion to a backward area. Like Americans a century later, they would learn after living in Vietnam that the country and its people had a distinct life and culture of their own that resisted change.

Several secret Vietnamese political or religious clubs, whose aims included winning independence for Vietnam, were formed in the 1920s and 1930s. They did not like each other, but they united against French rule. These

A Chinese street in North Vietnam.

Ho Chi Minh

Ho Chi Minh (born May 18, 1890, died September 3, 1969), president of the Democratic Republic of Vietnam (North Vietnam)

Who was he really? Was his name Nguyen That Thanh or Nguyen Ai Quoc? Actually, what he was called is unimportant. Ho changed his name several times during his life, usually to throw enemies off his tracks.

The thin young man was born in central Vietnam and attended school before sailing to France. He worked there as a teacher and in a photo shop.

Ho even made a brief voyage to the United States, where he washed dishes in a New York City restaurant. Returning to France, he began to work for Vietnamese independence. Soon he became a socialist and later a communist.

Ho formed the Indochina Communist Party in 1930, even though he had not been in his own country for 20 years. Traveling to the Soviet Union and then to China, Ho was jailed by the Chinese in 1941 as Japanese troops occupied Vietnam. The Vietnamese revolutionary finally talked his captors into letting him go. He went to Vietnam and met with Viet Minh soldiers.

In September 1945, Ho appeared in Hanoi to declare Vietnam independent. The French had no intention of giving up Vietnam, and the First Indochina War was soon under way. Ho became the leader of all the communists and some noncommunists. He inspired the people to keep fighting so that the French, the United States, and the South Vietnamese could be defeated. Ho died in 1969, six years before North Vietnamese soldiers entered Saigon to unite the country. Opinions differ about Ho's personality and his true feelings about politics. Everyone agrees that he was a valuable symbol to the North Vietnamese and the Viet Cong.

organizations searched inside and outside Vietnam for a leader. Many turned to a frail activist who called himself Ho Chi Minh.

Ho was born in central Vietnam in 1890. He used so many false names during his early years that few people remember what he was

A Vietnamese bazaar during French rule in the 1920s.

called by his parents. As a young man, he referred to himself as Nguyen Ai Quoc, which means "Nguyen the Patriot." He received a French education in the ancient city of Hué before setting off to travel abroad.

He visited China, Russia, Europe, and the United States, where he worked in a New York City restaurant. Ho took simple jobs as he studied and wrote about unifying Vietnam and achieving its independence. Even though he had not been inside Vietnam for 20 years, he founded the Indochinese Communist Party in Paris in 1930. Ho returned to Vietnam permanently in 1941, prepared to lead his people against the French.

He found that World War II had brought new masters to Indochina. The invading Japanese had turned his country—and most of Southeast Asia—into a colony of their own. The Vietnamese sought aid to fight the Japanese throughout World War II. After Japan's surrender in Saigon on September 12, 1945, the Vietnamese asked for assistance to prevent the return of the French. Significantly, the two countries

American GIs celebrate the end of World War II.

Hanoi during communist occupation, 1954.

they most often approached for foreign aid were China and the United States.

Neither country was in a position to listen. China had been heavily damaged by the Japanese. After the war it was torn apart by fighting between its corrupt government led by General Chiang Kai-shek and the Chinese communists led by Mao Zedong. The U.S. owed Ho Chi Minh a debt from World War II. Ho's followers, known as the Viet Minh, had rescued a number of American pilots whose aircraft had crashed in Vietnam or Laos. The Viet Minh saved these pilots

Rice fields glow in the afternoon sun near Quang Tri, central Vietnam.

from being captured by the Japanese, whose forces were being bombed by U.S. planes based inside China.

By 1946, the United States was tired of war. More important, the country's attention was focused on rebuilding Europe. This area was the birthplace of most American ancestors and the site of rapid expansion by Soviet Russia. France was one of the European countries offered U.S. aid. The French used some of this money to rearm their troops and to regain control over their colonies in Indochina.

Although at this point in the story we're more than 40 years away from present-day Vietnam, already we've reached a point where opinions differ. Did the United States make a mistake in supporting the French when they returned to Vietnam? Are we always responsible for the use of U.S.-made arms by another country? Should we automatically oppose communism in all cases? Or should we furnish more food and fewer guns to countries with major problems? In the coming chapters we'll explore answers to these important questions.

Chapter 2

The French Return

The French weren't the first Europeans to return to Indochina after World War II. The United States and its allies thought it would be best if friendly forces showed up quickly after the Japanese surrender. As a result, British soldiers were sent to southern Indochina to establish law and order. Chinese soldiers were also asked to help keep the peace, but they caused as many problems as they prevented.

The Chinese nationalist troops were half starved and ill clothed. They were weak from fighting the Japanese and the Chinese communist army. They stumbled toward Hanoi, stripping the countryside of food, clothing, and anything else they could take with them. The helpless population watched and wondered if any foreign power would ever treat them well or even withdraw and leave them alone. Here was a good reason to support Ho Chi

Minh: he wanted foreign soldiers out of the country.

President Roosevelt, before his death in the spring of 1945, warned Americans not to support the French if they returned to Southeast Asia. Roosevelt felt colonies would cause everyone trouble in the future. On the other hand, the British, led by Winston Churchill, believed France had the right to reclaim its colonies. The French did return, and with good reason. For more than 60 years, the countries called Indochina had produced important raw materials. Many French businessmen and government officials in Laos, Cambodia, and the three Vietnamese states lived like kings.

When the French first came to Indochina, 80 percent of the Vietnamese could read. When the French left, 80 percent of the local population was illiterate. French schools were not open to all Vietnamese, and public schools were

General Henri Navarre decorates a paratrooper at Dien Bien Phu.

World War II allied leaders (from left) Winston Churchill, Franklin D. Roosevelt, and Joseph Stalin. Roosevelt wanted France to give up its claim to Indochina.

neglected. The natives had few rights. They were often held in prison for long periods without being charged with a crime. Some were worked until they died. Death often resulted from such diseases as malaria or tuberculosis, or from malnutrition. Some French landowners lived in villas with 30 rooms while their laborers and servants lived in huts with dirt floors. Life was no better for the Vietnamese in 1945 than it had been in 1885.

A few Vietnamese, about 6,000 among 20 million, became wealthy under the French. Likewise, Chinese immigrants who moved to Vietnam often became rich middlemen. They offered farmers very little for their crops, then sold the crops overseas for large sums. There was no middle class and most people had no hope of improving their lives. The Vietnamese wondered how this could happen. Wasn't France the country where the phrase "liberty, equality, brotherhood" once sparked a revolution? Yes, but laws that were obeyed by the French in their own country were ignored by them in Vietnam.

Just how mistreated were the Vietnamese? As an example, a widespread disease once killed almost all of the water buffalo. The plague ruined many farmers, who depended on the big, gray beasts for plowing. Yet even after the animals were dead, the French continued to demand taxes on them! French authorities also taxed everything from rice wine used in religious ceremonies to table salt. The only way to avoid big debts was to move away to another part of Vietnam. Yet it was hard for people to leave because they loved the land where their families had lived for centuries.

Life was no better under Japanese rule during World War II. At first, the Vietnamese greeted the invaders happily— they liked seeing Asians in control. The Japanese promised to improve conditions, but by the end of the war, thousands of Vietnamese had starved to death; the Japanese had forced them to give most of their crops to the wartime government. As the Japanese withdrew, Vietnamese who had cooperated with them were attacked and often killed by starving villagers.

After the Japanese were defeated, Ho Chi Minh emerged from his jungle hideout in North Vietnam to declare Vietnam independent in a memorable speech on September 2, 1945. His phrases sounded familiar to the few Americans in the crowd. It turned out the revolutionary's words were taken from the Declaration of Independence! A copy of the historic document had been given to Ho by a U.S. intelligence officer. What Ho did not say was that he had made up his mind to let the French return if the Chinese would agree to leave. He traded life under the Chinese for life under the French, who came back to reclaim their colonies early in 1946.

What kind of man was Ho Chi Minh? American intelligence officers in Vietnam at the time all agreed he was capable and shrewd. He spoke French, English, and a Chinese dialect, in addition to Vietnamese. He knew history, economics, and current events, and could inspire his countrymen. The Americans also believed that Ho was a schemer, a revolutionary, and a communist. Americans who met him, however, usually felt that a self-governing Vietnam was more important to Ho than communism. Perhaps they hoped for a capable person to run Vietnam, and Ho seemed very capable.

Meanwhile, in the South, events were just as complicated. The British established military law in Saigon, where a few American intelligence officers had arrived to look after U.S. prisoners of war they might find. The British were having trouble with several Vietnamese religious groups. Earlier, the Japanese had allied themselves with various religious leaders in the South, promising them each a role in the government after the war. They did this to keep southern Vietnam peaceful and hopeful. After the Japanese were driven out of Indochina, members of the Cao Dai sect and other religions became angry at the prospect of living under French rule again. The French had become even less popular during World War II. Some of them who had stayed in Indochina during the war had made fortunes selling addicting drugs such as opium and heroin. For years, the French had run a

American servicemen land in New York City after World War II.

profitable drug trade out of Indochina, a trade not even a world war could stop.

The opium poppy, grown in mountainous areas of Indochina, also helped raise money for arms for Ho Chi Minh's soldiers, the Viet Minh. Ho worked with Vo Nguyen Giap, leader of the guerrilla army. Like Ho, Giap was from central Vietnam. An intelligent man and a revolutionary since his teens, Giap worked as a school teacher while he urged the Vietnamese to fight the French. If he hated the French, he had good reasons: Giap's wife and son died in 1941 while being held in a French jail. Yet he respected French culture and spoke the language fluently.

Giap spent World War II recruiting members for the Viet Minh. When the war ended, he had about 1,000 armed soldiers in the North and hundreds of spies, informers, and guerrilla soldiers spread throughout Indochina. Much of the early equipment used by the Viet Minh was captured from Japanese, French, or Chinese soldiers. Additional arms were purchased with money obtained from the sale of opium poppies to drug processors.

Vo Nguyen Giap

Vo Nguyen Giap (born 1912), general and commander of North Vietnamese armed forces

Foreign Legionnaires almost captured Giap in 1947. That was not the only close call for this man, who was born in a rugged part of central Vietnam. A few years younger than Ho Chi Minh, Giap learned Ho's views while a law student and a school teacher in Hanoi. Giap saw in the struggle for independence a chance to be part of a historic military campaign.

Giap's Viet Minh forces suffered several defeats after World War II before the general decided to use guerrilla tactics. He taught his troops not to attack the French unless the French were outnumbered and outgunned. Even though Giap's wife and child died in a French jail in 1941, he liked French culture and admired Napoleon.

Giap was not a fan of the United States. His troops could be kind to wounded French soldiers but fought without rules against Americans. A man who could make and follow numerous plans at once, he was the person who directed the 1968 Tet Offensive. A military failure but a propaganda success, Tet almost wiped out the Viet Cong (communists from South Vietnam). The 1968 series of battles forced more North Vietnamese to come South to fight.

All sides in the war sold drugs to raise money for weapons, food, and supplies. The French sold opium to Vietnamese who could not afford to use drugs. Almost as bad, in the view of the Vietnamese, Frenchmen favored the Chinese minority who lived in Saigon. These "overseas Chinese" frequently made fortunes going back and forth as middlemen between the French and the Vietnamese population. When the Vietnamese people complained about the situation in 1945, the French turned on them, killing men, women, and children. After the war ended, the Vietnamese ransacked French homes, killing anyone they found. Death was even more common in the North, where an estimated two million people were dying of starvation and disease.

Ho was criticized by his followers for agreeing to let the French return. He was prepared for such criticism and told fellow Vietnamese that the French were finished in Southeast Asia. They would not be willing to endure a prolonged fight to stay in Vietnam. But the Chinese, he said, would never leave if they were permitted to stay. The thin leader with the

Harry S. Truman

Harry S. Truman (born May 8, 1884, died December 26, 1972), 33rd President of the United States

Truman became President after the death of Franklin D. Roosevelt in 1945. He was in charge of the country during the period from World War II through the Korean conflict in the early 1950s. He made several decisions that were important in Vietnam.

Truman believed communism should be contained. That is why America sent troops to fight in 1950 in Korea. The President felt that the French, who were fighting Vietnamese communists, needed help. He provided them with more than $2 billion in money and weapons while America fought Korean communists. Incidentally, Truman ordered the invasion of Korea without approval from Congress. Lyndon Johnson pointed this out later when he sent troops to Vietnam on his own. Also, Truman had ordered the atomic bomb dropped on Japan in 1945. During the Vietnam War, some Americans pointed to this fact when they urged the use of atomic weapons in Vietnam.

Many Americans disliked Truman while he was President. Self-educated and from rural Missouri, he was a man of strong opinions. No President ever had to make so many decisions that had such fateful consequences later on.

French troops question a Viet Minh suspect, 1950.

wispy goatee was 56 years old and barely recovered from malaria. He had no idea the communists would eventually run China, but he guessed correctly that Western forces were tired of war.

Meanwhile, war was the furthest thing from the minds of American soldiers. They were returning to U.S. farms, villages, and cities, getting married, learning trades, going to college, or starting families. The children born right after World War II were called "baby boomers." They greatly increased the population.

These hill people knew little about the French-Viet Minh war.

These tiny new citizens did not know that Vietnam would be a big part of their lives when they became young adults.

If Americans weren't concerned about warfare, their government was. President Harry S. Truman and his fellow Democrats wanted to prove they disliked communism. Many Democrats felt voters believed they were friends of communists. So Truman's advisers came up with a policy called "containment." This simply meant that the U.S. and its friends would prevent communism from spreading its influence anywhere on earth. They felt containment was necessary because they imagined countries around the world falling like dominoes to communism. In fact, any group of countries where revolutionary or communist movements existed were pointed to as an example of "the domino theory" at work. France received American money and weapons to fight in Vietnam because the U.S. wanted to prevent the fall of Southeast Asian nations to communist rulers.

Incidentally, it's not completely correct to call the colonial troops in Vietnam Frenchmen. They were a mixture of Africans, Asians, Europeans, and Middle Easterners, usually fighting because carrying a rifle paid more than anything they could do in their own countries. There was at least one other reason to be in a French uniform: many Germans joined the famous French Foreign Legion because they feared being imprisoned after World War II. There were numerous Africans in French ranks as well. This meant that Vietnamese saw black soldiers long before Americans came to fight in 1965.

North Vietnamese children with their water buffalo. Most peasants were more concerned with farming than with politics.

Chapter 3

War Once Again

The war between the French and the Vietnamese began on a seemingly peaceful note. In 1946 the French asked Ho Chi Minh to come to Paris and discuss Vietnam's independence. Ho left eagerly, full of hope that his country would finally be free.

Instead, while Ho was in Paris, the French formed a new Vietnamese government. They said that Bao Dai, a member of Vietnam's historic royal family, would lead Vietnam into the future. Ho and the Vietnamese all knew that Bao Dai would be a puppet ruler. That is, the French would tell him how to act and what to say. Although Bao Dai came from a line of kings, he had no talent for leadership and did not really want to run the country. In fact, he loved being away from Vietnam, traveling in Europe or going to night clubs in Hong Kong.

Ho Chi Minh, although angry at being tricked, did not want to start a war. He reluctantly signed a cease-fire agreement with the French and returned home. When news of the cease-fire became known, a few outraged Vietnamese troops attacked isolated French military posts, then retreated into the hills around Hanoi. Fighting also flared in Haiphong, where the French ordered Vietnamese soldiers to leave the port city. When the Vietnamese said the cease-fire agreement allowed them to stay, the French attacked. Infantry and armored units entered crowded neighborhoods while a French gunboat shelled the city from the harbor. Many historians believe this battle, in which some 1,000 Vietnamese died, signaled the start of the First Indochina War.

As the fighting grew worse, the French were given airplanes and weapons by the United States. Every time the U. S. complained about the cost of arms, the French

Ho Chi Minh felt he had been deceived by the French.

36

warned of a communist takeover in Southeast Asia. President Harry S. Truman did not want to go down in history as the man who helped lose Indochina to communism. So during his 1948-1952 administration, almost $2 billion in planes, weapons, ammunition, and money were given to the French. Add another $1 billion to this from the U.S. from 1952 to 1954, and you can see why this war half a world away gradually got the attention of the American public.

Few Americans knew that, from 1945 through 1950, the French lost 50,000 troops (the U.S. lost 57,605 in Vietnam from 1965 to 1973). Few single battles killed large numbers of troops. Instead, a few each day were wounded or killed in road ambushes, and by snipers, booby traps, mines, or mortars—portable tubes that fire small but deadly exploding shells. Nearly as many French soldiers died from disease and poor medical care as were wounded on the battlefield. The troops suffered from such tropical hazards as dysentery, ringworm, trench foot and trench mouth, rashes, insect and snake bites, and other discomforts. Added to these

woes were terrible heat, a monsoon (rainy) season lasting several months, thick jungles, and elephant grass ten feet high. Clothing rotted and tore apart if worn more than three or four days. Even cooler mountain areas were difficult places to fight a war.

Overall, French soldiers handled the hardships well. Gerard Fournot, who now lives in the United States, served in Vietnam from 1948 until 1951. As a paratrooper, he received better food, higher pay, and better equipment than ordinary foot soldiers. French paratroopers made many combat jumps, leaping from old German Junker airplanes. These airborne attacks were able to surprise the enemy just as U.S. helicopter assaults surprised them 20 years later. Fournot says his outfit was very spirited and conducted many raids on the Viet Minh. "At first, the enemy relied on booby traps," he says. "They had old stuff, but it kept getting newer."

Fournot's military career ended when he was wounded in an ambush near the Chinese border. He was rushed in a tiny plane to Hanoi, then taken back to France

Emperor Bao Dai and his wife. The emperor preferred Paris to Vietnam.

to recover. A friend of his, Roger Cestac, was an officer in charge of engineers. He points out that 100 of 500 men who graduated in Cestac's French military school class later died in Indochina.

Conditions weren't easy for the Vietnamese communist soldiers, called Viet Minh. They began the hostilities with old equipment and little money. Their survival the first few years depended on farmers and peasants who fed the rebels and hauled weapons to them as they hid in the hills. This friendship between the guerrilla fighters and the people was to be important throughout both wars, first with the French and later with the Americans. Things improved for the Viet Minh after 1949, when communists took over China. They gave the Vietnamese weapons captured in Korea, plus guns and ammunition from the Soviet Union and Eastern Europe. By the end of the First Indochina War in 1954, Vietnamese ground forces were as well armed as the French.

However, we shouldn't think that the Vietnamese did everything right and the French did everything wrong. General Vo Nguyen

French troops await the communists at Dien Bien Phu in March 1954.

Bao Dai

Bao Dai (born October 22, 1913), last emperor of Vietnam

Many people would like to be kings or queens, but Bao Dai was a man born to be king who did not want the job. Bao Dai (real name: Nguyen Vinh Thuy) was considered by some Vietnamese as the one to lead his people to independence. However he had close ties to the French and became known as a lazy man who did as the French asked.

Bao Dai became emperor in 1925. He wanted to modernize the country, but the French would not help him. The Japanese took advantage of his good nature. After World War II, he left his country to avoid being manipulated by either the French or by Ho Chi Minh and the communists.

The emperor returned to Vietnam in 1949 with the title of premier. He wanted to unify Vietnam but had little following. Eventually he gave up trying to resolve the nation's problems and tried only to enjoy himself. After the Viet Minh (communist Vietnamese) defeated the French in 1954, Bao Dai fled to France. His last political act was to name Ngo Dinh Diem prime minister of South Vietnam. Diem soon named himself head of state, and Bao Dai remained in exile in France.

Giap, the Viet Minh leader, did not at first see the importance of fighting a hide-and-seek war. He sometimes told his forces to stand and fight the French in a formal battle. When the Viet Minh did so, too often they were blown to pieces by French air power and artillery. Later the Vietnamese set ambushes, attacking the French only when French forces were greatly outnumbered. Most important, they struck at night when the French were in forts and the Viet Minh were free to roam. As late as 1952, however, Giap had not learned these critical lessons.

The French created outposts far into the Vietnamese hills that were surrounded and overrun. The Viet Minh picked them off one by one. As Viet Minh soldiers moved slowly but surely toward Hanoi, a French general named Jean de Lattre formed a daring plan. He called on French civilians to occupy Hanoi and Haiphong defenses. That let him face the Viet Minh with every soldier he had. The Vietnamese attacked near Vinh-Yen, where about 50 heroic African and pro-French Vietnamese were eventually overwhelmed after terrible bayonet

Hundreds of Vietnamese peasants carry supplies to the Viet Minh, 1954.

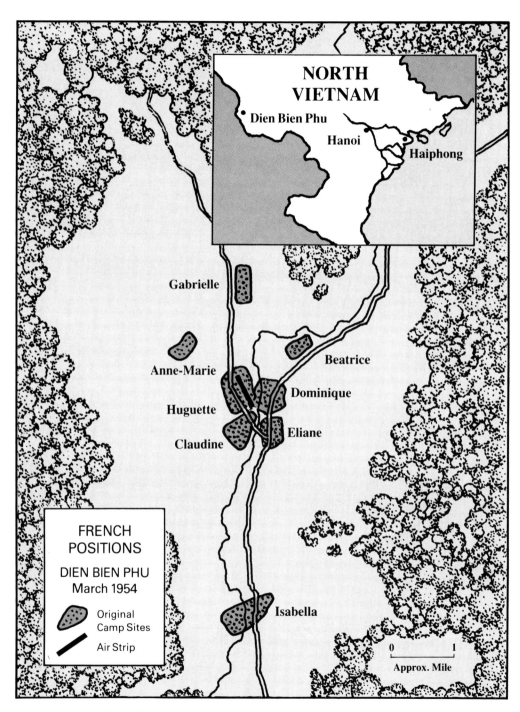

Dien Bien Phu was in a remote river valley in northern Vietnam.

A Saigon crowd demonstrates against the absent Emperor Bao Dai in 1955.

fighting. De Lattre then called in more troops and airplanes carrying napalm, the deadly jellied-gasoline bombs. Napalm burned hundreds of Viet Minh with each explosion. French troops survived human-wave attacks and the Viet Minh were thrown back. Giap lost 6,000 dead and 500 captured.

The Viet Minh returned to what had brought them success. Attacking by night whenever possible, they ambushed convoys, setting up additional ambushes to block French rescue forces. They continued to overrun isolated French forts and closed in on Hanoi. De Lattre died of cancer in 1952. His successor, General Henri Navarre, decided to pursue Viet Minh forces into the highlands. This led, in 1954, to an historic battle in a valley near the border with Laos. The valley was named Dien Bien Phu.

General Navarre is known for a phrase that became all too familiar in Vietnam: "Now we can see it clearly—like light at the end of a tunnel." He was speaking about victory over the communists at Dien Bien Phu. To do this, Navarre dropped paratroopers into the valley, then moved in

regular troops. These ground units were to be supported by artillery and by planes that would pin down the Viet Minh with napalm and other bombs. Instead, the Viet Minh overran the artillery sites, while fog prevented French planes from flying.

All through the spring of 1954, 13,000 French troops were attacked by at least 35,000 Viet Minh at Dien Bien Phu. The Vietnamese had hidden tons of artillery in the surrounding mountains. These big guns pounded French foxholes around the clock. When the guns weren't firing, the Viet Minh staged human-wave attacks. French soldiers threw them back again and again. Each time the circle around the French tightened. After weeks of fighting, the Viet Minh tunneled all around their enemies. The French could not see them but could hear them digging night and day.

French troops were told repeatedly that help was coming, but the dead and wounded kept piling up. A hospital plane was hit by mortars before it was able to take off with wounded men. There were dozens of new casualties every day. Many were

Dwight D. Eisenhower

Dwight D. Eisenhower (born October 14, 1890, died March 28, 1969), 34th President of the United States

Dwight Eisenhower was America's World War II military hero. As the supreme commander of Allied forces, he defeated German, Italian, and other Axis forces in North Africa and Europe. After serving briefly as a college president, he was elected President of the United States in 1952.

Eisenhower's main concern in Asia was Korea. He was able to negotiate a truce there in July 1953. He also made several decisions that affected Vietnam. The French, despite U.S. aid, were being defeated by the communists. A large French force was surrounded early in 1954 in a remote valley known as Dien Bien Phu. They pleaded for the United States to send troops and to bomb communist forces. After considering everything from a single air raid to dropping atomic bombs, Eisenhower said no to further assistance. French forces were defeated, in part because Eisenhower feared fighting the Chinese. Officials in

the Eisenhower administration helped negotiate the creation of two Vietnams, North and South.

This President has been accused of showing poor leadership and of letting the country run itself, but records prove his concern for foreign affairs. Shortly after John F. Kennedy was elected to succeed him, Eisenhower warned Kennedy of trouble in Asia. He was especially concerned about Laos. He believed America was too eager to settle things by sending in U.S. troops and using sophisticated weapons.

hidden in sandbagged bunkers below ground but received no medical attention. The Viet Minh dragged their dead and wounded from the battlefield as best they could. They were supplied by civilians who tied hundreds of pounds of food, medicine, and weapons to their bicycles then pushed the bikes over the mountains to the battle.

Meanwhile, high-level French soldiers and diplomats went looking for help. Their airplanes could not carry enough cargo to save the men of Dien Bien Phu, and they had few experienced soldiers left. They turned to the United States, because the U.S. had given them aid in the past. At that time President Dwight D. Eisenhower did not want to get U.S. forces involved. He believed China might join the fight on the side of the Viet Minh. Eisenhower had worked to stop the fighting in Korea, and he did not want another war. Without outside help, the outnumbered and outgunned French were doomed. They surrendered, and Viet Minh forces hoisted their red flag over Dien Bien Phu on May 7, 1954.

About 4,000 French troops died at Dien Bien Phu. Of the 9,000 who were taken prisoner, 2,200 died in a terrible 500-mile march to prison camps immediately after the battle. The Viet Minh lost many more men than the French, but were willing to lose men to win the battle. The French lost 75,867 soldiers between 1945 and 1954, with 10,000 men taken prisoner. Not one seriously wounded French prisoner survived prison camp. The Americans and South Vietnamese could have learned a lot from the French experience.

A cease-fire was declared after the battle, and the French began to leave Vietnam. Only three Americans had lost their lives in Indochina from 1945 through

1954. The first was A. Peter Dewey. He was an intelligence officer looking for Americans held by the Japanese in Saigon in 1945. Dewey was mistaken for a Frenchman at an ambush and was killed by machine gun fire.

The other two U.S. deaths took place during Dien Bien Phu. American adventurers James McGovern and Wallace Buford were flying supplies to the French when their Flying Boxcar was hit by ground fire. They crashed the big plane behind Viet Minh lines. Americans would continue to die in Vietnam over the next 21 years.

The Flying Boxcar of James McGovern resupplies a French outpost over Vietnam.

A. Peter Dewey, killed in 1945, was the first American soldier to die in Vietnam.

James McGovern, an American hero at Dien Bien Phu.

Chapter 4

The Country and the People

America and Vietnam aren't much alike today, nor were they much alike after the French defeat in 1954.

A visitor to Vietnam at that time would have noticed that the average Vietnamese was short and weighed between 70 and 120 pounds. He or she had straight, black hair and dark eyes and seemed very graceful to a much larger American. The Vietnamese language sounded to a foreign ear like the chirp and twitter of birds. Vietnamese is a tonal language. That means the same word can have half a dozen meanings, depending on how it is pronounced. If French sounded nasal and English came from the throat, Vietnamese sounded as if it were being sung. Even Americans who learned languages quickly had a tough time speaking Vietnamese, despite its Westernized alphabet.

Rural diets included rice at almost every meal, plus such vegetables as corn, sweet potatoes, yams, arrowroot, or soybeans. Duck, chicken, or pork were luxuries, but fresh or dried fish were eaten often. The Vietnamese dipped many foods in *nuoc mam*, a fermented fish sauce that smelled awful but had a mild, salty taste. This offered important nutrition if there were no meat, eggs, or fish at a meal. Tea was the national drink, with small cups of rice wine consumed occasionally. A rural Vietnamese family squatted or sat in the home around a square tray where the food was served. Each person had a porcelain bowl and two chopsticks. They scooped rice into the bowls and picked up meat or vegetables with the sticks. Bowls were held beneath the chin, and chopsticks were used to push rice into the mouth.

The Vietnamese were great snackers. That may have been

This Vietnamese man eats fish, a mainstay of the country's diet.

because no one liked to eat big meals in hot weather. They ate rice cakes and rice balls made from special, sticky rice. Other popular snacks were small meatballs (served on bamboo sticks), soybeans, cane sugar, noodles, eggs, fruit, and a breakfast soup made by pouring steaming broth over onions, noodles, and bits of raw beef. Some city dwellers ate French meals, such as bread, jam, and coffee for breakfast. City food reminded Americans of Chinese dishes, with a variety of tasty sauces, meat or fish, vegetables, and rice or noodles. Cookies and little cakes were very popular everywhere during holidays. Usually, there were a few snack sellers in every village. The large cities had street vendors selling all sorts of food and drink.

The cone-shaped hats thought of as Chinese were worn by Vietnamese farmers and villagers. These lightweight straw hats shielded the wearer from the sun. People in the cities who worked outside, and most rural Vietnamese, wore loose-fitting trousers and a shirt or blouse made of thin cotton or hemp. Since water was always near, san-

dals were worn because they drained and dried quickly. Some people who lived in cities dressed differently. Men working outside favored shorts and a light shirt. Other men dressed as we might — cotton pants, a short-sleeve shirt. Women wore dresses or pants and shirts, just as Americans, or they donned a lovely *ao dai* (pronounced *ow die*). The ao dai was a tunic that fit tightly and had long, silky panels in front and back. Worn with loose-fitting pants, the outfit was beautiful. Ao dais were not worn by women when they performed hard labor.

There were big differences between country and city homes. A village or rural home was likely to be made of bamboo, wood, straw, or mud, with palm leaves for a roof. The home was surrounded by a wall of greenery — banana, guava, or mango trees; shoots of bamboo; palm trees or hedge. All this gave the family privacy and kept the inside cool. Near the home were a vegetable garden and a water storage tank. Inside, the house was separated into a sleeping room, a living room, and a kitchen.

In cities, houses of the wealthy

Tilapia, a small fish often eaten in Vietnam.

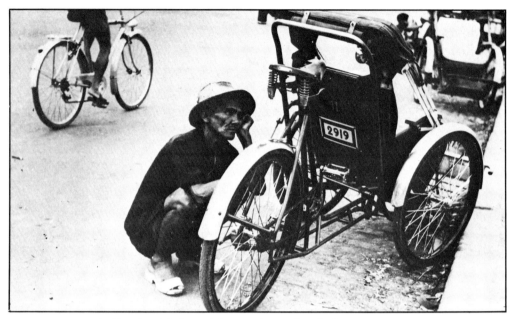

A bicycle rickshaw driver waits patiently for a customer.

or middle class were either large, old stucco homes built by the French, modest wood homes, or Chinese-style shophouses, with a store on the ground floor and living quarters behind and above. Fishermen all along the coast lived with their families on boats. Thousands of poorer city residents lived in cardboard boxes, under pieces of plywood, in drainage tiles, in huts made of old beer or soda cans, or on the street. Housing had been a problem for years in Vietnamese cities. Refugees fleeing the countryside in time of war made it worse.

Most Vietnamese were farmers or worked at farming as part of a family. The two big river valleys, one in the north and one in the south, produced more rice than the country consumed. Rice was exported to other countries, a trade that brought money into Vietnam — one of the poorest places in Asia. Men, women, and children worked in the rice paddies, plowing with a water buffalo and planting and harvesting by hand. Each rice paddy or field was surrounded by earthen fences called dikes. These dikes separated the rice fields and allowed

In Saigon fortunes were made selling goods, even currency, on the black market.

them to be irrigated. At harvest, the fields were drained for easier walking. There were wonderful new kinds of rice that could be harvested in 120 days. So three rice crops a year were possible in the hot, tropical climate.

A few industries existed. The Vietnamese made concrete, steel, plastic, paper, bicycles, small tools, and fabrics. One of the major exports was raw rubber, grown in plantations between the low paddies and the highlands. Forests of skinny rubber trees were completely unlike nearby palm plantations, where short, fat trees produced edible oil and other raw materials. Some ornamental flowers were grown for export in the highlands. Most mining took place in the north, where coal, iron ore, and other metals were found.

Since Vietnam was so close to the equator, there were only two seasons. Winter in the north was cool and dry, with temperatures of about 62° F in January. The south was very hot and dry in the winter. Both ends of Vietnam had hot and humid summers. Saigon's average annual temperature was 82° F, with readings well over 100° F common in the Mekong Delta and in other lowlands. Rain drizzled constantly in the north in February and March. The southern rainy season was from April or May to October and included heavy rains and high winds.

Except for the two ends of the country, there was little flat land. The mountains in some places ran from the border with Laos to the South China Sea. In other areas, a few rice paddies were found between the mountains and the sea. The central highlands were jungle-covered hills. The higher the hills, the cooler the temperatures.

About 700,000 primitive tribespeople lived in the highlands. They spoke many different languages and did not look like the Vietnamese. They were descended from early peoples who had lived along the coast but had been pushed into the hills as the Vietnamese moved south out of China. Known by various tribal names, these *Montagnards* (French for "mountain dwellers") also lived in mountainous areas of Laos, Thailand, and Burma. They were greatly affected by the war.

Mountains ranged from the middle of Vietnam northward. They weren't covered with snow, but they reached heights of 10,000 feet. Valleys between these mountains were foggy for weeks at a time and hid many troops. Other kinds of land included plateaus, sandy beaches, mangrove swamps, and low-lying deltas near big rivers. For its size, Vietnam had a considerable variety of landscape, much of it rugged and difficult to work.

Knowledge of the land, however, does not really reveal what the Vietnamese were like. American visitors found one major difference between them and the Vietnamese: Americans acted as individuals and Vietnamese acted as members of a group. Some experts traced this tendency back to rice farming, which is easier if done by groups of people. Further, the most important part of Vietnamese religious life was paying respect to ancestors. No matter what religion a Vietnamese followed, he or she probably had an altar for ancestor worship in the home. One of the reasons the Vietnamese were sad if forced to leave their homes was that many

A meal at a simple sidewalk restaurant. Chopsticks instead of silverware are used.

of their ancestors were buried in plots nearby.

Each Vietnamese had two or three names. The name Nguyen Ly had the family name first and the given name second. It is as if an American were asked her name and said, "Smith Anne." About half of all Vietnamese had the family name of Nguyen, and most people used one of only a dozen Vietnamese family names. In a large group, there were likely to be people who had the same family and given name. Middle names usually showed whether the person was male or female. Some Vietnamese changed their middle names several times during their lives.

Education was always important to the Vietnamese. The French did not know how much it angered the native Vietnamese when they were not allowed to go to school. A feeling for education came from the Chinese belief in Confucianism. This ancient, semi-religious philosophy stated that education led to good government. It taught believers to admire and respect teachers and public officials more than warriors, merchants, or anyone else. Even Vietnamese without many years of school knew the proud history of their country. Every child grew up learning the songs and poems that taught Vietnam's historic legends.

Adults always married—unless they joined a religious group. Families were large and children well cared for. Americans or Frenchmen who thought the Vietnamese were calm never saw them when their children were injured or in danger. A calm outward appearance, together with modesty, good manners, a soft voice, and humility—these were all considered proper behavior by the Vietnamese. On the other hand, being bossy or bragging or making fun of someone were considered terrible ways to act. Perhaps the Vietnamese calm, even during frightening moments, puzzled Americans more than anything. It was certain that their very different cultures and languages made it hard for Vietnamese and American troops to ever know each other.

Vietnamese women and children hide from fighting early in the war.

Chapter 5

Changes Here, Changes There

The period from the end of the Korean War to the beginning of the Vietnam War, 1953 to 1965, seemed to be a happy time for many in America. There was at least one new sound called rock 'n' roll coming over the airwaves. It was played on the radio and performed on the new consumer craze, television. The music was tremendously popular because, said a black musician, "It was white boys playing black boys' songs."

If all was well with middle-class, white Americans, however, black people were having a hard time. Segregation (laws that forced blacks to use separate and usually inferior public facilities) was the rule. In the South, where most blacks lived, they could not sit where they chose on buses or use most drinking fountains or order a meal in many restaurants. All this began to change in 1954, when the U.S. Supreme Court ruled against separate but equal schooling for whites and blacks. From then on, all American public schoolchildren were to receive the same education from the same teachers in the same schools. White parents in parts of the country protested and frequently enrolled their children in private schools. The protest reached such a furor that, in 1957, federal troops were sent by President Dwight D. Eisenhower to enforce school integration in Little Rock, Arkansas.

Integration, shown on television, had an incredible impact on the American public. White people, sitting in their living rooms, saw innocent blacks beaten and abused. TV network news, showing frightening film footage, rallied support for black and white civil rights workers and blacks in search of public education. In the

Black and white Americans participate in the historic March on Washington, 1963.

late 1950s and early 1960s, all sorts of racial barriers came crashing down. No more seats for blacks only in the rear of buses. No more separate public rest rooms or drinking fountains. No more serving blacks only in the kitchens of restaurants. If a black person had the money, he or she could eat lunch wherever it was served.

Integration proved that Americans didn't really like injustice. It also showed how powerful a persuader television could be. The first generation of children raised with television in their homes were more sympathetic and tolerant of black people. They were also active. By the summer of 1963, young blacks and whites marched on Washington. Their stated theme was the belief in equality and justice for all. The theme that was not stated was this: "We have energy, we hate whatever is unfair, and we won't automatically follow or defend every government decision." Not even the death of a hero, in this case President John F. Kennedy, stopped this wave of young American activism.

This same period in Vietnam was equally unusual. Yen Do, who now lives in California, remembers Saigon in 1954. "I was a high-school student then. I had been part of an anti-French nationalist resistance network in the schools. But after the French government left, I could not tell the nationalists from the communists. It was confusing."

Yen Do and others knew that the one million Roman Catholics who migrated from the North were anticommunists. They were fleeing brutal northern land reform. Trying to give the landless peasants farm land had cost the lives of many innocent northerners whose only crime was that they owned some land themselves. Nevertheless, thousands of southerners went North because they believed in Ho Chi Minh and his victorious army. The line marking the border between the two new countries of North and South Vietnam had been drawn by Vietnamese and French politicians in Geneva, Switzerland. Both sides promised to hold democratic elections within two years to try to unite North Vietnam and South Vietnam into one country.

Federal troops enforce school integration in Little Rock, Arkansas, 1957.

Bao Dai, South Vietnam's emperor, named Ngo Dinh Diem prime minister—even though Bao Dai stayed in France on the Riviera! Diem returned from Paris to run South Vietnam. He faced many problems. Yen Do points out that Diem's biggest success came against several warlords. These men were the leaders of strange religions (one included Charlie Chaplin in its list of saints) or of large and well-armed gangs. They demanded a share of power. Diem had one warlord beheaded in public and bribed another into following the new prime minister. Unfortunately, many followers of these warloads joined communists operating south of Saigon in the Mekong Delta.

Diem named himself chief of state, which meant that Bao Dai was stripped of power. Almost every American official who met Diem believed he was a poor leader. Diem had a large police force and several armed forces generals behind him. He cracked down on communists and non-communists alike. In many cases, his tough tactics actually made people more sympathetic to the com-

Ngo Dinh Diem

Ngo Dinh Diem (born January 3, 1901, died November 2, 1963), president of the Republic of Vietnam

A tragic figure, Ngo Dinh Diem was an honest man who could not see dishonesty when it was close to him. Born into a Roman Catholic family in central Vietnam, Diem was trained by the French as an administrator. He took an instant dislike to communism and, in 1933, was named to a government position. However, his open dislike of French rule cut short his government career.

Diem, who never married, lived and worked quietly until 1942, when the Japanese took control of the country. He asked them to make Vietnam independent, an action that caught the eye of Ho Chi Minh. During World War II, communist guerrilla troops captured Diem, who turned down an offer to join Ho.

Luckily, the guerrillas set him free.

After World War II, Diem became an enemy of communism and traveled as far as the United States for aid. He was named prime minister of South Vietnam in 1954 and hoped to keep the new country independent. However, everything Diem did seemed to make enemies. He was unfriendly and trusted no one but his family and friends. He upset Buddhists and all other non-Catholics. He angered Americans who tried to help him. He even had to face demonstrators who thought he was soft on communism!

Meanwhile, the communist National Liberation Front (called the Viet Cong) gained strength in South Vietnam. Diem and his brother, Ngo Dinh Nhu, were overthrown and killed in 1963 by anti-communist South Vietnamese military officers.

Ngo Dinh Nhu

Ngo Dinh Nhu (born 1910, died November 2, 1963), political adviser to his brother, Ngo Dinh Diem, who was Vietnam's president

A complex man, Ngo Dinh Nhu came to be more feared and hated than his brother, Diem, who ruled Vietnam from 1954 until both were shot to death in 1963.

Nhu told Diem what to do, and Diem often followed his brother's advice. An emotional man, Nhu could yell at a reporter one minute and then lapse into long periods of almost trancelike silence. There were rumors that he was a drug addict and that he had a hand in the drug business in Saigon. He saw himself as a great political philosopher—but he invented a philosophy called personalism that no one understood. Nhu was either unwilling or unable to talk about it. It appeared to be the exact opposite of communism, but no one knew for sure.

Nhu eventually turned the Vietnamese military and the government against each other. He organized many informers to prevent his brother from being overthrown. During the early 1960s, no one dared trust anyone else. Political and military leaders became much more open and at ease after Nhu's death.

munists. With land reform used as an excuse to kill in the North, and with politics the excuse in the South, all of Vietnam was a dangerous place to be.

There were other problems. Diem's family, led by his brother Ngo Dinh Nhu and the brother's wife, Madame Nhu, were well known and disliked by almost everyone. Nhu was said to be involved in the drug trade, a multimillion-dollar business at the time. He invented a strange philosophy he called personalism. It was his answer to communism, but hardly anyone understood it.

Madame Nhu pushed for stronger government control over everything from daily newspapers to street peddlers. The Nhus and Diem believed that everyone who opposed them was a communist. No wonder the 1956 elections promised by Diem to reunite the country were never held.

Meanwhile, the United States had poured hundreds of millions of military and development dollars into South Vietnam. Although U.S. officials were not happy with Diem, he was America's best hope at the moment to prevent communism from taking over the South and possibly moving into Laos, Cambodia, Thailand, Malaysia, Burma, and Indonesia. As America pumped in money and equipment, well-trained communists infiltrated from the North. Their job was to take over the country, village by village. This was done peacefully where the village headman agreed and violently where there was resistance. These takeovers, coupled with terrorist bombings that ripped through Saigon, let country resident and city dweller alike know that the National Liberation Front, as the

Madame Ngo Dinh Nhu

Madame Ngo Dinh Nhu (born 1924), South Vietnamese political activist

This woman is so amazing, it's hard to know what to call her. She was married to the brother of Ngo Dinh Diem. Diem ruled South Vietnam from 1954 to 1963. She saw herself as the country's first lady, since Diem was not married. Many people, inside and outside Vietnam, thought Madame Nhu was at best strange and at worst crazy.

Born in Hanoi of wealthy parents, she dropped out of high school to marry Nhu in 1943. She spoke French at home and spoke but never learned to write Vietnamese. A pretty woman, Madame Nhu embarrassed the shy Vietnamese with her blunt remarks and strange, flamboyant behavior. After the deaths of Diem and her husband at the hands of military men, she accused America of helping with the plot. She went on a speaking tour of the United States in 1964 but failed to rally support for herself and her family in South Vietnam. The widow who saw herself as a heroic figure soon faded from the headlines.

General Maxwell Taylor (in dark glasses) inspects fortifications during a 1961 visit near the demilitarized zone.

Viet Cong political arm was called, was alive and on the march.

President Eisenhower's second term ended in 1961. At that time there were 700 American advisers in Vietnam. It was their job to train the South Vietnamese to use modern weapons and to teach them how to match wits with the enemy. Newly elected President John F. Kennedy sent an increasing number of advisers and expanded their role. Military men returned from Vietnam saying publicly that the Viet Cong were on the run. In private, they reported that the South Vietnamese civilians didn't care who was in power as long as the people were allowed to go about their business. Even worse, they whispered, South Vietnamese soldiers were as bad as the Viet Cong were skilled. After visits by Vice President Lyndon B. Johnson and General Maxwell Taylor, Diem asked for more money and advisers so that he could increase the size of his army. Since there were 100,000 South Vietnamese in uniform (against only 20,000 Viet Cong), Kennedy decided against sending in U.S. ground forces, as Taylor

John F. Kennedy.

had suggested. He did provide more civilian and military advisers, which soon totaled 12,000.

Some Americans who were sent to Vietnam as advisers began to take an active part in the war. Covert (secret) operations were launched. They were hidden from the press and the public because U.S. forces were only supposed to train, not fight. But Vietnam did not lend itself to such clear-cut distinctions. A good example is the Green Berets.

Special Forces, as the Green Berets were officially known, have been thought of as President Kennedy's idea. However, the first Special Forces unit arrived in Saigon during the Eisenhower administration in 1957. Their task was to train Army of the Republic of Vietnam (ARVN) soldiers, then to develop a counterinsurgency, or antiguerrilla, program. By 1960, Green Berets were scattered in isolated villages across the country, training villagers to defend themselves. Usually about a dozen Green Berets moved into a village, bringing arms, medicine, and technical know-how. These men fortified remote villages, especially those where

Special Forces soldier with a snake.

Montagnards (mountain-dwelling tribes) lived. When the Viet Cong saw the success of the program, they often attacked. The Special Forces fought to defend themselves.

From 1960 to 1962, Special Forces units teamed up with the Central Intelligence Agency (CIA) to fight in Laos. Thinly populated with primitive people, Laos is a land of jungle-covered hills. Mountain tribes grew opium to trade for salt, iron, or tobacco. Into the mountaintop world of the Hmong and other tribes came the Special Forces. They were highly trained in guerrilla warfare and survival skills. A team of a dozen—two officers and ten enlisted men—won the confidence of the tribes by treating their injuries and diseases. They lived among the people, giving them modern rifles and other small weapons and teaching them how to defend villages against communist attack. They also taught patroling skills, and joined tribespeople to fight the enemy.

Since no one could carry crates of rifles over Laotian mountains, the CIA created an airline, Air America. Pilots, packers, and "cargo kickers" were found, trained, and paid well to fly slow-moving cargo planes over foggy, damp jungles to isolated outposts. This secret war went on because the United States believed North Vietnamese were trying to take over Laos.

While many Vietnamese cut through Laos on the Ho Chi Minh Trail, there's no indication that they were fighting Laotians. Rather, the fight was an internal one. Pro-American, pro-communist, and neutral Laotians eventually decided to run the country together, but this agreement did not last. Several years later, when U.S. forces entered Laos, they found that Americans had already fought—and died—in this lonely land west of Vietnam.

By 1962, South Vietnamese adopted a tactic that was new for them. Instead of waiting for the Viet Cong to strike, the army used American helicopters and armored personnel carriers to chase the enemy. The helicopters in particular were effective. They were a flying platform for arms, with their rockets and machine guns. At first, the enemy tried to hide or shoot at the choppers with rifles

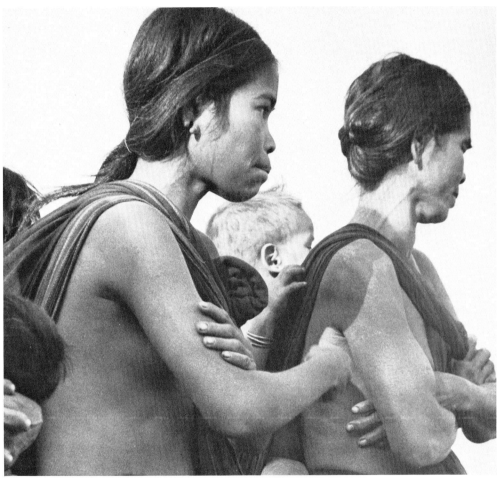

Montagnards were hardy allies of the Green Berets.

or small machine guns. U.S. and Vietnamese pilots learned to fly above 3,000 feet, which was out of accurate rifle range, or to stay at treetop level to avoid being easily seen.

The South Vietnamese and their American allies were to go unchallenged in the air. But the Viet Cong had several advantages on their side. One was terror. Terrorism can take many forms. With National Liberation Front (Viet Cong) guerrillas, it included:

• A roadblock where friends were allowed to pass and enemies

Rebel troops and civilians at the Presidential Palace in Saigon, 1963.

were killed.

• The destruction of a big-city restaurant where foreigners and Vietnamese alike were killed or injured. A powerful bomb could be attached to a parked bicycle and triggered to blow up the building.

• A kidnapping, often of a son, daughter, or wife of a village headman who had not been as cooperative as the Viet Cong wished.

• Assassinations of village leaders and other political figures who refused to work with the Viet Cong.

• A booby trap placed where an American soldier would trip it, causing him to lose an arm, a leg, an eye, or his life.

Once South Vietnamese indicated that they either favored the Viet Cong or were passive, the VC treated them well. In contrast, when Diem's soldiers entered a village, they mistreated people, then drove off. The Viet Cong showed up as night fell and talked earnestly and politely to the people. It was not hard to understand why, even with tons of new weapons, the South Vietnamese were not winning the war.

Chapter 6

The End of Diem

President John F. Kennedy's administration had problems with foreign policy. The missile crisis with the Soviet Union and the half-hearted Bay of Pigs invasion of Cuba clearly showed the administration's weaknesses.

Would Vietnam be different? Kennedy certainly had plenty of intelligent staff members. Secretary of Defense Robert F. McNamara, for example, came to Washington after a brilliant career as head of Ford Motor Company. The President's younger brother, Robert, was smart and aggressive. Others came from college teaching jobs, research organizations, and the worlds of business and government. These people studied Vietnam as hard as any government ever studied anything. They ended up with failing grades.

In 1962 President Diem undertook a "strategic hamlet" program, an approach he copied from Britain's experience in Malaysia in the 1950s. British and Malaysian forces defeated 12,000 communists in that country by moving entire villages into well-protected areas. Without village support, the guerrillas were eventually defeated. Diem's strategic hamlets were key towns where Vietnamese could be moved a safe distance from the Viet Cong. Despite failure of an earlier, similar program, the South Vietnamese plan received the backing of the Kennedy administration.

From the outset the program was riddled with problems. Diem's forces had the habit of creating a strategic hamlet in an area where the VC still operated. As a result, the site became one more place where the Viet Cong had supporters. Many villagers were moved far from their farm land, which they needed to earn a livelihood. Also, ARVN soldiers tended to stay in the strategic hamlets instead of pursuing the

President Diem seemed ill at ease with both Vietnamese and Americans.

enemy into the countryside. Residents of the new hamlets were forced to help build watchtowers and fortifications after working long hours in nearby rice fields.

The strategic hamlet program came to be ridiculed by U.S. military advisers and soon was forgotten—except by the press. Questions from reporters about this and other errors annoyed American volunteers who had tried to make the program work and irritated their supervisors in Saigon and Washington.

Since Vietnam was hardly a democracy, Diem could do whatever he pleased to the press. At first he ignored them; but when foreign reporters wrote unflattering stories about Diem and the government, the president was annoyed. He complained to Washington and was astonished to learn that Washington was not in charge of U.S. reporters or other foreign correspondents.

It turned out that the ruling Ngo family was its own worst enemy. Madame Nhu, the wife of Diem's brother, strutted around Saigon, making a fool of herself with her demands and opinions. Her antics were reported to the

Henry Cabot Lodge

Henry Cabot Lodge (born 1902, died 1985), Ambassador to Vietnam

Tall, handsome, and from one of Boston's most famous families, Henry Cabot Lodge played an important role in Vietnam. Lodge was U.S. Ambassador when unhappy Vietnamese military officers killed President Ngo Dinh Diem in 1963. Lodge told the officers that America would not interfere with their plans. If the military men thought the U.S. approved of removing Diem from office, they were right.

Lodge quit as Ambassador in 1964 to find out if America wanted him to be a presidential or vice presidential candidate. He had run for Vice President in 1960 with Richard Nixon. The two Republicans were barely beaten in 1960 by Democrats John F. Kennedy and Lyndon B. Johnson. Kennedy first nominated Lodge as Ambassador, a post he held in 1963-1964 and again in 1965-1967. In 1969, Lodge was appointed chief negotiator for discussing peace with the North Vietnamese in Paris.

Lodge first visited Vietnam as a reporter in the 1930s. He gave advice on Vietnam to two Democratic Presidents and one Republican President.

world. In retaliation, Diem's police and military forces closed several Vietnamese daily papers and continued to complain about foreign reporters to Washington.

If the press made any errors at that time, it was failure to cover the unusual conflict going on in Laos, Vietnam's neighbor to the west. Information was hard to get in this mountainous country. The confusing fight taking place among communists, noncommunists, and neutrals was not reported for several years. Yet this backward, sparsely populated nation was to play an important part in the eventual outcome of the Vietnam War.

Reporters and U.S. advisers alike were amazed in January 1963 when Viet Cong forces not only stood up to but defeated a large Vietnamese force. When ARVN units landed in helicopters near the village of Ap Bac, west of Saigon, VC were waiting for them. The enemy shot down five large choppers, then ambushed Vietnamese troops in open fields. Neither artillery, air strikes, nor armored personnel carriers could dislodge the Viet Cong from tree-lined, fortified positions. They

Villagers found life in strategic hamlets difficult.

A Saigon crowd cheers at the destruction of a statue that resembles Madame Nhu.

continued to pour in a hail of bullets from all sides.

When night fell, 200 Viet Cong silently walked out of a poorly laid trap set by more than 2,000 ARVN soldiers with their space-age weapons. South Vietnamese soldiers were at the mercy of their leaders, who were more likely to be friends of Diem than to be experienced, capable officers.

Diem by this time had few remaining friends. Two Vietnamese pilots lobbed bombs into the Presidential Palace one morning in 1962. It was a clear indication that the military was growing tired of Diem's rule. The ranks of the Viet Cong were swelling, though the exact number was difficult to know. Many American civilian and military advisers told anyone who would listen that Diem and Nhu were stumbling blocks on the road to creating a free country. The strangest and most frightening form of protest, however, was to come from Buddhist monks and their followers.

Buddha's birthday is as important to Buddhists as Christmas is to Christians. When a Catholic archbishop in the city of Hué told Buddhists they could not fly their

religious flags, the Buddhists protested vigorously. Government troops clashed with the protesters, shooting and killing nine people. Buddhists demonstrated again when the government accused protesters of being Viet Cong. In June 1963 a Buddhist priest shocked the world by burning himself to death while seated on a Saigon street. This act brought more criticism of Diem than he had ever experienced before.

Diem, as usual, handled this incident poorly. He said other Buddhists had drugged the priest before he was set afire. Madame Nhu dismissed the affair as a "barbecue." Nevertheless, Diem reluctantly signed a list of demands the Buddhists gave him. He and the Buddhists both knew such a paper was meaningless—Diem would not keep his word. Other Buddhist monks—and at least one nun—burned themselves to death to protest government actions. Diem's solution was to stage bloody raids on 2,000 Buddhist pagodas and temples in August. The Kennedy administration was amazed at the Vietnamese government's lack of sensitivity to public opinion.

Buddhist priests, called *bonzes*,

Followers react as a Buddhist monk burns himself to death to protest Saigon government corruption.

were not supposed to be worldly. Yet they handled the press much better than did the government, taking time to explain that the self-burnings were the furthest thing from suicide. The acts, they pointed out, created martyrs and showed the severity of the problem. One Buddhist monk even offered U.S. officials this advice: either force Diem to make democratic changes or get rid of him. Since Diem and the Nhus would not reform, the United States decided to oust them. They chose an unlikely man for the job.

The new ambassador to Vietnam was Henry Cabot Lodge. He had run unsuccessfully against Kennedy in 1960 as Richard Nixon's vice presidential mate. Kennedy wanted him to straighten out the mess in Vietnam. This was a large order, since Kennedy's own staff was split on whether Diem should be overthrown and if so, who should lead the country. Lodge made contact with a group of unhappy military officers, then told Washington what everyone suspected: the war could not be won as long as Diem ran Vietnam.

Lodge finally got the officers moving on November 1, 1963.

The anti-Diem forces launched an attack on the palace with mortars, planes, and automatic weapons. Diem and Nhu fled through a secret tunnel to the home of a friend. From there, Diem demanded that the generals put down their arms. He and his brother even made a desperate, last-minute attempt to contact North Vietnam for some sort of help. Instead, the military captured the brothers as they sought safety in a nearby church. Later that day, Diem and Nhu were shot to death inside an armored personnel carrier.

The North Vietnamese were amazed that the U.S. would help overthrow Diem. They worried more about the Americans than about which Vietnamese was in charge of the South. Communist leaders knew the Viet Cong were performing well against the poorly trained and badly led Vietnamese, but Americans forces were a different matter. If the opportunity came, would North Vietnamese soldiers stand and fight against the Americans with their bombs, rockets, and artillery? The answer would come, but not for almost two years.

Tanks surround the Presidential Palace after Diem's downfall.

John F. Kennedy

John F. Kennedy (born May 19, 1917, died November 22, 1963), 35th President of the United States.

Elected in part because of his intelligence and sense of humor, Kennedy was America's first Roman Catholic President. He was a wealthy Democrat who was highly successful with domestic concerns but less skilled abroad. He worked with many people who were considered experts in foreign and domestic affairs.

These experts did not always give Kennedy good advice. For example, two of his advisers told him to send combat troops to South Vietnam but to tell the public that they were there to prevent floods! Kennedy allowed America's military presence in Vietnam to increase from less than 1,000 to more than 12,000 during his presidency.

The President was not blind to the faults of the South Vietnamese. He agreed with his advisers that President Diem was not good for Vietnam, and he knew long before it happened that South Vietnamese military men planned to overthrow Diem. Kennedy was killed by an assassin, Lee Harvey Oswald, on November 22, 1963, before he could make major decisions affecting the U.S. presence in Vietnam.

Americans were upset when Diem and Nhu were murdered. But three weeks later the murders were overshadowed when an assassin's bullet killed President Kennedy on November 22, 1963. The President had told several people at different times that he was going to pull all U.S. advisers out of Vietnam after the 1964 presidential election. Numerous Kennedy aides said he was especially unhappy that Americans had played a part in Diem's overthrow and murder.

Vice President Lyndon B. Johnson was sworn in immediately after the assassination and promised to carry on Kennedy's programs. In meetings before and after Kennedy's death, LBJ, as he was called, took note of the conflicting messages coming from Southeast Asia. He found that when any two experienced and intelligent men presented their views on the situation, those views often would be completely different! Johnson may have known from the start that there were no certain answers about Vietnam.

American President John F. Kennedy is shot in Dallas on November 22, 1963.

Chapter 7

America Edges Toward War

Lyndon Baines Johnson's first year in office appeared to be a dream. There was popular support for his Great Society domestic programs, which provided better housing, a new interstate highway system, a greater number of jobs, and other benefits. Americans supported Johnson, because they knew he had had the job of President thrust on him unexpectedly. They proved their support by re-electing LBJ in a landslide victory over Barry Goldwater in 1964. Goldwater made the mistake of being too warlike on Vietnam. LBJ wisely assumed the role of keeping young Americans out of a land war in Asia. The public was not aware of the impact Vietnam already had made on the former senator from Texas.

After taking office in November 1963, Johnson could have accepted President Kennedy's plans regarding Vietnam. Instead, he let several Kennedy advisers persuade him not to withdraw U.S. helicopter pilots from Vietnam. His decision was based on fears that Americans would blame Democrats if Vietnam ever became a communist state. He felt we needed to keep supporting South Vietnam in its struggle.

For a moment, the government of South Vietnam seemed to be headed in a good direction. Saigon residents were wildly happy that the Ngos were gone. They celebrated the end of Madame Nhu's power with music and dancing, two forms of entertainment she had banned. Prisons released Vietnamese whose only crime was opposition to Diem. Clive Curran, now living in the Los Angeles area, was in the U.S. Army in Saigon in 1963. He remembers: "Saigon was sort of fun. We were told to stay out of certain parts of the city. But any big city has dangerous areas. Saigon was cheap and the food was great. I never

Vice President Lyndon B. Johnson succeeded President Kennedy.

saw much trouble."

Many of the problems around Saigon were not readily seen. As the war in the country escalated, more and more refugees left their traditional homes and came to the capital. These capable farmers found they could make more money washing clothes or shining shoes for Americans than they could growing rice. Yet because Saigon prices were much higher than in rural areas and always rising, the refugees could not afford a permanent place to live. They could be seen everywhere—living in the rubble of a construction project, in a wrecked car, or in cardboard boxes. Sanitation did not exist and diseases spread.

The only good aspect about this migration was that it deprived the Viet Cong of potential recruits. As families left villages, the Viet Cong recruited more and more women. American advisers who captured these soldiers assumed they were nurses for the enemy. But VC females did much of the same work as the males. In contrast, the main problem for young women in Saigon and elsewhere was a lack of single men. Vietnamese marry early, then work

Two Saigon women take a stroll in their *ao dais*.

Lt. General Minh.

Maj. General Khanh.

and have children. In Saigon, with three single women for every man, girls had to get jobs. Gradually, the best things a single Saigon girl could bring to a marriage were a good job, a bit of money saved, or a wealthy family.

At this time, there was talk among leaders in Saigon of forming a neutral government. This was an unusual proposal coming from supposedly warlike military men who had overthrown the president. South Vietnamese neutrality was a view advanced mainly by the French. They owned rubber plantations and other businesses and still had influence in Vietnam. American diplomats and advisers believed a neutral approach would let the communists easily take over.

Yet the group of generals in Saigon didn't seem to want to run the country. General Duong Van Minh, an unusually tall Vietnamese, told American reporters that he liked playing tennis and tending his garden better than governing. Minh was ousted in January 1964 by General Nguyen Khanh. A stubby man with a goatee and high blood pressure, Khanh had no more leadership qualities than the man he replaced. Robert McNamara, Secretary of Defense, visited Vietnam and confirmed not only that South Vietnam was losing the war but that it was losing it at a faster rate than before Diem was killed. McNamara did not tell the public about his thoughts, but other Americans spoke out.

U.S. advisers from throughout Vietnam were writing home to friends and relatives, telling anyone who read their letters how poorly the Vietnamese performed as soldiers. They lost more weapons to the enemy than they captured. They refused to patrol at night. When fired upon, they either did not fire their own weapons or fired weapons on automatic, spraying wildly. Even worse, they treated innocent villagers with contempt, and they stole food. They tortured the few prisoners they managed to capture. On operations, they either brought their wives and children along with them or else went home whenever they felt like it. They were a complete contrast to the enemy.

How could two men from the same village, one a member of ARVN and one a Viet Cong, behave so differently? A Vietnamese who now lives in Orange County, California, thinks he knows: "Americans taught the South Vietnamese that they could always rely on U.S. help. The Viet Cong—and later on, the North Vietnamese—had no one to intervene on their behalf. So they fought very well. Also, South Vietnam had little time to organize as a nation. Should they think of themselves as Vietnamese or South Vietnamese?" There was never any doubt among the Viet Cong that they were Vietnamese and that their goal was a reunited, independent, and communist Vietnam.

American advisers at first underestimated the enemy. Then, as things continued to go well for the VC and badly for the South Vietnamese, advisers thought the enemy was perfect. They were as human as anyone else, but they worked harder and planned more carefully. Each Viet Cong mission was well rehearsed, with scale-model villages or ambush sites used to show every guerrilla where to be and what to do. This precise planning enabled the

U.S. Secretary of Defense Robert McNamara (wearing glasses) during a 1963 visit to Vietnam.

enemy to bury mines and to put booby traps in place. In the event that Vietnamese and U.S. advisers came at the Viet Cong from an undefended direction, the mines made a great defense.

Mines were not always what they appeared to be. A mine used on a highway often was a stolen ARVN artillery shell, buried just beneath the road and just above a nail. A human, even an ox cart, could pass over the shell without harm, but a heavy truck or a tank would detonate the shell. If an ambush was planned and no mine was available to stop a convoy of trucks, the VC patiently cut down a large tree to block the road. Once the ambush was sprung or the mine exploded, fleeing soldiers had worse surprises awaiting them in the jungle off the road.

Three kinds of enemy booby traps are shown. At left, a misstep can cause a grenade to explode. Top, a spiked bamboo rod. Bottom, a thin wire that sets off a hand grenade. All three were used by Viet Cong guerrillas.

Booby traps and antipersonnel mines came in several forms. A common booby trap was a hand grenade with a wire wrapped around the pin. A soldier tripped the wire, which pulled the pin. Since the grenade went off several seconds later, it wounded men in front of and behind the blast. There were buried antipersonnel mines, too. One type made a sickening click if stepped on. As soon as the foot moved, the mine went off. Other mines were hidden among weapons, food, or supplies, waiting for ARVN soldiers to grab them. The most deadly were "command detonated." These mines were set off by a concealed enemy soldier who pulled a wire trigger when someone came near the mine. Handmade booby traps included bamboo spikes in a pit, or logs with spikes that dropped from overhead on soldiers walking on the trail below.

Viet Cong soldiers traveled much lighter than their ARVN counterparts. The VC could do so because they hid or buried supplies where the packets could be quickly recovered, or they could find food in most villages. A VC soldier typically carried a satchel of rice, a rifle, no more than a few dozen bullets, perhaps a grenade and a rolled-up hammock for sleeping above the jungle or swamp floor. They were country boys fighting city boys in a country war. ARVN soldiers always

looked overloaded—with metal helmets, flak jackets, heavy boots, and belts with various pouches and packets of food and ammunition. ARVN members (or Vietnamese marines or paratroops) were dressed so that they could survive being hit by a bullet or by shrapnel (flying metal from a bomb, artillery shell, grenade, or mine). Viet Cong simply planned not to get hit in the first place.

By 1964, the guerrillas were challenging the idea that they

U.S. troops hitch a ride. There were no communist tanks early in the war.

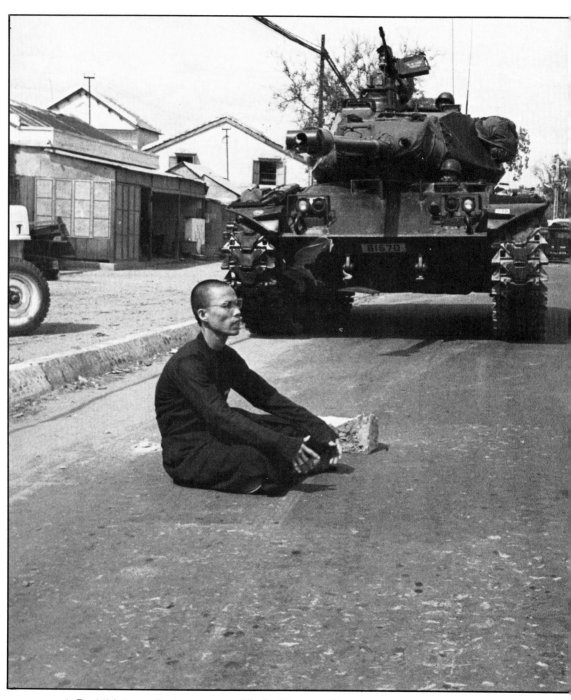

A Buddhist monk stops war traffic in Danang. Buddhists protested government corruption throughout the country in the 1960s.

never fought a conventional battle. Taking advantage of what one reporter called "a cascade" of different leaders in Saigon, the Viet Cong went looking for a fight. They found several in the winter and spring of 1964, from the Mekong Delta to the Cambodian border. Each time, U.S. advisers found ways to trap and defeat the guerrillas. Yet these victories were not easily won. American advisers often had to take over command of the battles. Time after time, South Vietnamese military leaders failed to place their troops properly or to show up as planned. They allowed many VC to slip away from carefully laid traps.

Secretary of Defense Robert McNamara reported to Congress that the VC "have made considerable progress" since Diem's overthrow. He sent 5,000 more American advisers to Vietnam, putting 21,000 on duty there by mid-1964. In response North Vietnam began to send experienced leaders and more weapons and supplies down the Ho Chi Minh Trail.

This conference in Geneva, Switzerland, in 1954 split Vietnam into two separate countries.

Chapter 8

War North, War South

The Demilitarized Zone was a narrow strip of land on either side of the 17th parallel that crossed Vietnam's midsection. This line dividing North and South Vietnam had been established half a world away in Geneva, Switzerland, in 1954. Representatives of three countries—Canada, Poland, and India—were to make sure that the DMZ, as it was known, stayed free of troops and fighting. Canada represented democracy, Poland represented communism, and India was the neutral country.

The plan failed miserably. Soon after the DMZ was created, it became a virtual crossroads for both sides. South Vietnamese went through the DMZ on their way north to join Ho Chi Minh. As more American advisers arrived in South Vietnam, guerrilla forces trained in the North came South across the zone. In 1964, North Vietnamese Army (NVA) regular soldiers hiked across the DMZ to fight.

Lacking any heavy industry, North Vietnam's best resource was its people. They carried, pushed, or pulled south tons of supplies provided by China and the Soviet Union. Weapon-filled ships docked at the port of Haiphong, North Vietnam, every day. North Vietnam became a huge warehouse for a war being fought as much as 1,000 miles away. The combined strength of thousands of individuals has never been more amazing. Living on tiny amounts of food, soldiers and civilians alike hauled heavy burdens from ports to highways to trails, traveling perhaps ten miles a day. Invisible from the air, the Ho Chi Minh Trail and other paths had once been used for opium delivery by highland tribes. Now they were keeping Viet Cong forces clothed and supplied with food and arms. The trails also were pathways for propaganda.

North Vietnamese propaganda specialists (called political cadres) came south to keep Viet Cong (and later NVA) spirits high. While hiding in thick jungle between battles, enemy soldiers were taught that the U.S. was like France: it wanted to rule all of Vietnam. The jungle fighters were told repeatedly that Vietnam had to be one country because the Vietnamese were one people. Soldiers became convinced of this message, then passed on the message to villagers. The soldiers also believed that their side was morally right. Thinking about this view of the war helped many Viet Cong and NVA troops survive terrifying air strikes and artillery bombardments.

In Washington, President Lyndon Johnson was meeting with dozens of civilian and military advisers. Military men wanted the U.S. to be tougher. Most of them advocated bombing the North—up to and even including the use of nuclear weapons. While nuclear arms were seriously considered only by extremists, military and civilian experts drew up plans to bomb the North long before the plans were needed.

Lyndon B. Johnson

Lyndon B. Johnson (born August 27, 1908, died January 22, 1973), 36th President of the United States

No President ever started a term with more support. Former Vice President Johnson was propelled into the office of President by the 1963 assassination of John F. Kennedy. He sponsored the great civil rights legislation of the 1960s and promoted many social programs to build a "Great Society." Yet in less than four years the country was split over Vietnam. In fact, there was so much disagreement about the war that Johnson decided not to run again for President in 1968.

Lyndon Johnson was a school teacher who became a U.S. Senator and a friend of President Franklin D. Roosevelt. A tough-talking Texas Democrat with a big heart, he brought calm to the nation after Kennedy's death. His strengths showed in his domestic programs; his weaknesses showed in how he dealt with Vietnam.

Johnson sent jets to bomb military targets in Hanoi in 1965. Later that same year, he ordered United States troops into combat in South Vietnam. Before the Marines waded ashore in Danang, only U.S. advisers had seen any action. Johnson kept sending more American soldiers and did not know how to stop the escalation. His advisers were loyal, but because they had originally worked for Kennedy, Johnson was never sure they could be trusted.

He became less sure—and more angry—when Kennedy's brother, Robert, decided to run against him for President. Robert and several other Democrats had come out against the war. An angry and war-weary Johnson surprised the country on March 31, 1968, by declaring that he would not seek re-election. He died in 1973, less than a week before the signing of an agreement to end the war in Vietnam.

Some civilians argued that the U.S. should simply hold the line, neither escalating nor pulling out troops. For a time this view won out. It seems today to have been the worst possible choice, since Viet Cong and North Vietnamese Army regulars were increasing their attacks. In fact, by 1964 most Special Forces were already experiencing rugged fighting against communist troops. In that year President Johnson stepped out of a strategy meeting to award the war's first Medal of Honor to a Green Beret captain.

By late 1964, Special Forces in teams of 12 were spread all over South Vietnam and Laos. They were most often found along the Vietnam-Laos or Vietnam-Cambodia borders, living with Montagnards or other minorities. These American jungle fighters trained the natives to defend themselves against Viet Cong attacks on their villages. The hill people were easily trained and were fierce fighters. They disliked all Vietnamese, since Vietnamese had always mistreated them. The Montagnards led Special Forces to the enemy along trails known only by the mountain people. The American public was not aware of this secret war, especially since there weren't supposed to be U.S. troops in Laos. Some American officials did know about the secret war, however. One was William H. Sullivan, the U.S. ambassador to Laos, who coordinated air strikes on the Ho Chi Minh Trail. He worked with CIA-hired civilian pilots flying Air America planes into Laos and Cambodia.

Southern forces were not supposed to be operating in North Vietnam either. But groups of Vietnamese, trained by the U.S.

Navy at several Pacific bases, were raiding North Vietnam in small, high-speed boats. These covert (secret) missions began after another type of operation had failed. The U.S. had tried parachuting small groups of South Vietnamese into North Vietnam, but these raids produced few results—except the deaths of the South Vietnamese volunteers.

At the end of July 1964, the United States sent the destroyer *Maddox* to patrol off North Vietnamese waters in the Gulf of Tonkin. Its job was to wait for the South Vietnamese raiders to be picked up by North Vietnamese radar. The *Maddox* was then to check the radar to see how good enemy defenses really were.

On the night of August 2, three North Vietnamese patrol boats traded fire with the *Maddox*. The U.S. ship outgunned all three patrol boats and dodged enemy torpedoes. Two nights later, in stormy seas, the *Maddox* and another U.S. destroyer thought they were coming under attack again. Actually, no enemy ships were in the area. The *Maddox* captain later admitted that bad weather could have fooled both ships into think-

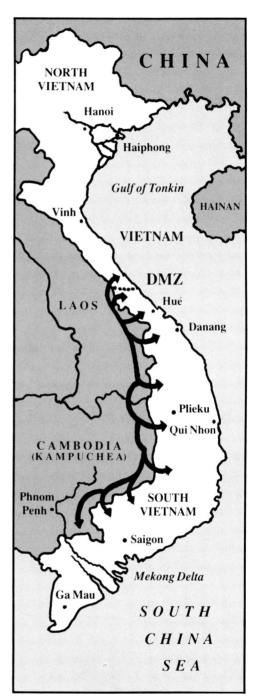

Arrows mark the routes Viet Cong used to invade South Vietnam below the DMZ.

The *Maddox*, a U.S. Navy destroyer.

ing the enemy was approaching.

However, the captain's first report about the August 4 "attack" was relayed to headquarters. Within an hour, the U.S. Pacific fleet told President Johnson that two destroyers in the Gulf of Tonkin had been fired on by North Vietnamese patrol boats. Johnson ordered 64 Navy jets to hit North Vietnam targets that the military had already selected.

Launched from carriers at dawn, the aircraft hit oil-storage tanks and patrol boats amid heavy fire. Two planes were lost. This air strike, Johnson told the country, was required because of attacks by the North. Only years later was it revealed that no August 4 battle with the North Vietnamese had ever taken place.

The entire event was very important at the time, however.

Immediately afterward, President Johnson asked Congress to pass the Gulf of Tonkin Resolution. It gave the President many powers to respond quickly in a warlike situation. The resolution passed the U.S. Senate by a margin of 88-2. A dozen senators wondered about giving the President so much authority, but ten of them joined the majority. Helping to secure the vote was Senator William Fulbright. Only two years later, the Arkansas Democrat would change his mind and become one of the leading critics of the war.

Several groups who ended up being against the war were showing their concern. Church members were heading for Vietnam, not to convert Vietnamese to Christianity but to help them in their daily lives. Among the most active were American Friends Service Committee members. Sponsored by the Quakers, these dedicated people patched up anyone who was hurt on either side of the war.

They also made artificial limbs and braces for all Vietnamese. Their efforts were small compared to U.S. Agency for International Development (USAID) programs. Best known for handing out tools during the unsuccessful strategic hamlet program, USAID

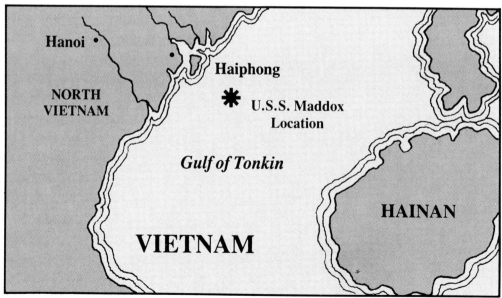

The Gulf of Tonkin, east of North Vietnam.

provided millions of dollars in manpower, brainpower, and everything from rice to radios. The program also included medical care, medicine, and weapons. The weapons were provided to villagers so they could defend themselves. Hundreds of USAID civilians were running the program in Saigon at the time of the Gulf of Tonkin incidents.

Attacking North Vietnam opened a wound that has not healed to this day, because many U.S. pilots remain missing in action. One of the two pilots whose planes were shot down survived the ordeal. Navy Lt. Everett Alvarez, a Californian, was flying an A-4 Skyhawk jet from the aircraft carrier *U.S.S. Constellation*. Alvarez and his fellow pilots ran into heavy antiaircraft fire that hit his plane. He ejected, but the fall and landing in shallow water broke his back. The pilot became the first of 600 airmen to be held in the "Hanoi Hilton," an old French prison. Alvarez survived eight years as a prisoner of war.

As Americans raided the North, South Vietnamese leaders were bickering over who should run the government. General

Lt. Everett Alvarez, the first prisoner of war in the Vietnam War.

Maxwell Taylor, the new U.S. ambassador, tried to sort it all out. Catholic, Buddhist, and student activists in Saigon held demonstrations as Americans wondered: How bad would the war get before the South Vietnamese all got on the same side? Not all his advisers agreed with President Johnson's immediate halt to the bombing after the August 5 raid. Yet most of them supported the war and tried to get the South Vietnamese and Americans to work together. One who was a team player, through good times and bad, was

General Maxwell D. Taylor, right, wears a bullet-proof vest during a helicopter inspection tour. The door gunner checks his M-60 machine gun.

General Maxwell D. Taylor

General Maxwell D. Taylor (born August 26, 1901), U.S. Army General, Ambassador to Vietnam

General Maxwell Taylor was President John F. Kennedy's idea of the perfect soldier—he wrote books, he was intelligent, and he was a graduate of West Point. Taylor was also a World War II airborne hero. He was Army Chief of Staff and, in 1962, became chairman of the Joint Chiefs of Staff, the nation's highest military job.

Taylor served as Ambassador to Vietnam in 1964 and 1965. Surprisingly, he was against bringing U.S. ground troops to Vietnam to fight. He knew that American advisers and the Vietnamese weren't winning against the Viet Cong. He believed Southeast Asia did not suit the American soldiers' fighting methods. He favored bombing North Vietnam.

Resigning the Ambassador's job in 1965, the General continued to give President Lyndon B. Johnson advice through 1968. After the war, Taylor said he believed the U.S. had jumped into the situation in Southeast Asia without knowing all the facts. That, he said, had been a dangerous thing to do.

General William Westmoreland. He assumed command of all U.S. troops but tried his best to stay away from Saigon's politics.

Westmoreland had his hands full. Since the North Vietnamese had a small air force, they could not fly south to strike back. Instead, they sent more NVA troops down the Ho Chi Minh Trail. The Viet Cong, having been bombed and shot at by American pilots for several years, contributed greatly. VC soldiers staged their first mortar attack on an American airbase at the end of October. They destroyed five bombers at Bien Hoa before getting away without a casualty. This nighttime attack, a dozen miles from Saigon, showed that VC strength had increased. It also indicated how the enemy intended to stop the bombing.

Actually, President Johnson had decided even before his great election victory over Goldwater in 1964 to greatly limit bombing the North. He wanted to hit North Vietnamese targets only when the VC or NVA launched a major ambush or attack. This decision was a difficult one for the President. A man who had always

Bomb-laden U.S. Navy Skyraiders take off from a carrier.

rounded up support for a cause, he found his advisers disagreeing on almost every situation that came up. The more Lyndon Johnson was forced to make decisions by himself, the more angry, brooding, and depressed the President became.

Since President Johnson launched the first offensive against the communists, is he to blame for U.S. involvement in Southeast Asia? He is no more at fault than any other President. A total of six Presidents were in power during the 30 years of conflict, 1945 to 1975. Perhaps Johnson's major mistake was not just his decision to continue the war. It may also have been trying to create great social programs at home while fighting a war on the other side of the globe. President Truman decided in 1946 that supporting the French was in our interest. Everywhere else, we supported local people over colonial rule. From that point on, each President forced his successor to make more difficult decisions about Vietnam. Unfortunately, Lyndon Johnson's decisions came during a time of great social unrest in the United States.

Antiwar demonstrations increased in size as the conflict continued.

Chapter 9

Hearts and Minds

A group of students meeting in Port Huron, Michigan, in 1962 was to have great symbolic impact on the war in Vietnam. These were college boys and girls who met to form what came to be known as the New Left.

American politics has tended to be split into leftists and rightists. Leftists believe the government should help solve problems. Their opponents are rightists, who believe that the government should stay out of peoples' lives. Leftists tend to sympathize with the poor, the uneducated, and the blue-collar worker. Rightists tend to sympathize with small and large business owners and managers, and the more wealthy people. Extreme leftists, like extreme rightists, want to use force if necessary to change things. Some of these leftists are communists. Left-wing politics nearly died out in the U.S. after leftists in the 1930s allied themselves too closely with the communists. By 1962, however, all true communists in the United States were old and inactive, and the communist party was nearly nonexistent.

The students meeting in Michigan wanted a new society—free of the past and supported by workers—that would resolve some of the country's chronic problems. Not many of their ideas were ever widely adopted. But these Students for a Democratic Society (SDS) were often out front in the antiwar movement. Since radicals usually were from either the East or West Coast, these New Left sons and daughters of middle-class Midwesterners were something new.

SDS members joined California's Free Speech Movement and other radical groups on college campuses, promoting many causes. They staged demonstrations to protest what they saw as lack of personal attention to their

Pham Van Dong, North Vietnam's premier.

An SDS member addresses the crowd during a
demonstration at Harvard University.

needs at large universities. The war, with its impersonal draft system, soon became a new target of protests. A national program was created by SDS for the 1965-66 school year. When some schools tried to head off trouble by banning SDS before it even was formed, students at those colleges immediately started chapters. The organization itself was very idealistic but had little to offer besides a lot of energy. Social programs were thought up but never tried; idealistic slogans were dreamed up but had no ties to peoples' real lives. The New Left never did receive much support from workers. Ironically, it was workers—and their sons—who would end up being drafted to fight and die in Vietnam.

The draft was a method of making sure the country had as many soldiers as the government wanted. In the 1960s, males who became 18 years of age had 30 days to register for the draft with their local Selective Service office. Registration provided them with a draft card that they were told to carry at all times. The card identified the bearer as having signed up for the draft, and it gave him a

A Vietnamese woman replants foliage after American soldiers cut down rubber trees that could conceal the enemy.

classification. There were about 20 different classifications. If the young man was a student, he was classified II-S. This meant he had been granted a deferment, or delay, so that he could complete high school, college, vocational school, etc. Upon leaving school or graduating, the student had to inform his local draft board so they could change his Selective Service status. A classification of 1-A meant the person could be drafted and possibly sent to Vietnam if he passed a physical examination. Women were not subject to the draft.

There were many ways someone could become eligible for the draft. A married man 25 or under frequently received a I-A reclassification if he got divorced. While men convicted of a violent crime were classified as unfit for service, those convicted of nonviolent crimes were offered military duty instead of prison.

Students and others who received a I-A status tried many ways to stay out of the service. Some worked at failing their military physical examinations. Young men from wealthy families could evade the draft by being

Boys attack a draft card burner in Boston.

An American Navy bomber takes part in the escalation of the war over central Vietnam.

named as member of a company's board of directors or by vacationing in Europe until the war ended. A common way for less well-to-do men to avoid military service was to admit to drug use or membership in either a white supremacy or black militant group. Hundreds also became pacifists, briefly or permanently.

In late 1964 and early 1965, the world awoke each morning to find out if yet another group of military men had seized power in Saigon. The Viet Cong took advantage of this instability and staged a number of costly attacks in terms of lives lost and weapons destroyed. Ranging throughout South Vietnam, the enemy wiped out hundreds of ARVN soldiers and killed dozens of Americans. Many of the U.S. dead were noncombatants, including aircraft maintenance soldiers in a four-story concrete barrack. In a daring daylight attack, the Viet Cong set a powerful explosive in the concrete structure, and the blast collapsed the building. Twenty-one of the 43 soldiers in the barrack were killed.

Americans retaliated with air strikes, hitting various North Vietnamese targets in a series of raids dramatically named Rolling Thunder. Pilots returned from these missions telling of intense enemy antiaircraft fire. Virtually every military target in the North was ringed with antiaircraft weapons from Russia and China.

All pilots feared being shot down, but they were well equipped if that happened. After ejecting from his disabled plane, a pilot had a strobe light that signaled his location to rescue helicopters waiting off the coast. In addition to a two-way radio and a pistol, the pilot also had a survival kit. In it were matches, flares, dye (for use if the pilot fell into the sea), an inflatable raft, and more. If he landed in a rural area, he had a good chance of being found by the rescuers in their helicopter. Major hazards included injuries from the force of ejecting at hundreds of miles an hour, the impact of hitting the ground, or attack by civilians.

While being a pilot was not easy, neither was it easy to protect the huge airbase at Danang from attack by the enemy. President Johnson made the final decision to send American troops to Viet-

American soldiers tour Saigon in bicycle rickshaws.

nam to improve protection of the Danang base. Too often, in supposedly safe places such as nearby Pleiku, South Vietnamese soldiers had allowed the enemy to sneak past them in the night. These suicide squads carried satchels of explosives. Johnson and his advisers feared that a satchel, placed near Danang's vast quantity of fuel, could wipe out the entire site.

On March 8, 1965, 3,500 U.S. Marines landed on the beach at Danang, rolling onto the shore in special landing vehicles. Not knowing what to expect, the Marines carried their rifles ready. They were greeted under a warm, hazy sky by local officials and girls dressed in silky *ao dai* outfits. As artillery and tanks were made ready for battle, the girls gave the soldiers flowers and smiled shyly. This welcome amazed the Marines, who would find that the only sure thing in Vietnam was the unexpected. Famed for their

Americans found Pham Van Dong to be stubborn and shrewd.

fighting ability, the soldiers were told that they would be given nothing but guard duty for the first few days. Nevertheless, the United States had sent its first fighting men to Vietnam. The undeclared war against the North had begun.

Ambassador and former General Maxwell Taylor remained upset at the prospect of American troops doing the actual fighting in Vietnam. On March 28, the ambassador left Saigon for Washington. He was optimistic to reporters, but he was so impatient with all the South Vietnamese governments that he yelled at a group of high-ranking Vietnamese military men. As it turned out, Taylor left at the right time. The U.S. embassy was hit by a VC explosive, hidden in a car, on March 29. The explosion blew out the embassy's windows, shattering the glass into dangerous, flying fragments. Two dozen people, including several South Viet-

THANKS TO THE U.S. GOVERNMENT AND PEOPLE FOR THEIR DETERMINATION IN PROTECTING FREEDOM IN V.N

namese in the street, were killed instantly and many more were injured. This is the kind of war it would turn out to be. Death could come on a busy street, a lonely trail—or behind a desk.

What did the rest of the world think of Vietnam? The Soviets were competing with the Chinese for North Vietnam's friendship. The Soviet Union wanted a friendly port in Southeast Asia, where the presence of their navy would make China and the U.S. nervous. There is also some evidence that the Soviets wanted the United States to get bogged down in a land war. In places like Korea, the Philippines, Thailand, and Australia, American allies were being asked by the Johnson administration to send forces to Vietnam. Southwest of Vietnam, Indonesia was in the midst of civil disturbances. Unlike the problems in South Vietnam, the Indonesian civilians and military were rising up against the communists. Indonesian communists, who were often of Chinese ancestry, were brutally slaughtered. As many as five million may have died. It was a terrible way to prove that the "domino" in the domino theory could fall both ways.

Meanwhile, the Marines extended their influence outside Danang. They went on the offensive, rooting out suspected Viet Cong and keeping villagers on edge. Wives and children of military and U.S. government personnel were told to leave Vietnam. They were unhappy at the order, because life was inexpensive and pleasant if you were careful. More and more reporters, photographers, and camera crews got off planes in Saigon. They hoped to get exclusive stories that might propel them to the top of their newspapers, radio, or television professions. Civilian engineers completed assignments and headed for home as the military took command of the American presence in Vietnam.

In North Vietnam, women and children were sent out of the cities. Factories were closed and moved from Hanoi and Haiphong to villages, jungle areas, or caves. Young men from throughout the country were ordered to report for military service. They left, knowing they might never see their families again. Food had to be imported, since the South no longer traded factory goods for its

U.S. Marines are greeted by children as they roll into Danang.

U.S. soldiers came to regard Southeast Asia as a confusing and depressing place.

rice surplus. Women, wearing conical straw hats or tropical army pith helmets, took on important roles. They fired antiaircraft guns, they repaired bombed bridges, they planted and cultivated and harvested. President Ho Chi Minh was in failing health and no longer ran the government. Decisions were made by Premier Pham Van Dong. From the start, Dong refused to be forced by the bombing to end the war.

Some 25,000 more soldiers joined the Marines in Vietnam in April 1965. They were told, as all American troops would be told, that they had been sent to Vietnam to "win the hearts and minds of the Vietnamese people." The average age of U.S. combat soldiers in Vietnam was 19. These young men knew nothing about Southeast Asia and cared little for the people. Most sergeants, captains, and colonels who led them subscribed to the theory that "If you have a man by the throat, his heart and his mind will follow." This habit of treating the native population as the enemy was to contribute greatly to the eventual fall of South Vietnam.

Timeline of Vietnam: 3000 B.C. to 1988

3000 B.C. The people we call the Vietnamese begin to migrate south out of China.

100 B.C. Start of China's 1,000-year rule of Vietnam.

A.D. 938 Vietnam becomes independent.

1500 The first European explorers visit Vietnam.

1640 Alexandre de Rhodes, a French Roman Catholic missionary, arrives in Vietnam.

1744 Vietnam expands into the Mekong Delta. The Vietnamese by this date rule over all of present-day Vietnam.

1844 The French fleet destroys Vietnam's navy.

1859 Saigon falls to the French.

1883 The French capture Hanoi.

1930 Ho Chi Minh starts the Indochinese Communist Party.

1939 The communist party is outlawed in Vietnam.

1941 The Japanese take control of Vietnam as Ho Chi Minh returns from a Chinese prison and the Viet Minh (communist army) is founded.

1945 Ho Chi Minh declares Vietnam independent as the Japanese surrender.

1946 The French return, and the Viet Minh take to the hills as the French Indochina war begins.

1952 Viet Minh forces are defeated several times by the French.

1954 The French are defeated at Dien Bien Phu and agree to leave Vietnam. Vietnam is divided into north and south following a cease-fire agreed upon in Geneva, Switzerland.

1955 The U.S. begins to send aid to South Vietnam.

1956 President Ngo Dinh Diem refuses to hold elections, as had been promised in the Geneva agreement.

1957 Communist guerrilla activities begin in South Vietnam.

1959 The North Vietnamese start to send soldiers into South Vietnam.

1963 The Viet Cong (South Vietnamese communists) defeat regular South Vietnamese soldiers at Ap Bac. This is the first major battle between the two sides. Buddhists protest South Vietnamese government policies. President Diem is overthrown and killed by the military.

1964 North Vietnamese patrol boats attack an American destroyer in the Gulf of Tonkin. Congress gives President Lyndon B. Johnson special powers to act in Southeast Asia. The first American pilot is shot down and taken prisoner by the North Vietnamese.

1965

1965 American air raids take place over North Vietnam. The first American combat troops arrive in South Vietnam.

February 7 Viet Cong attack U.S. bases. President Johnson replies to the attacks by bombing targets in North Vietnam.

March 8 The first American combat soldiers—3,500 Marines—arrive in Vietnam to guard Danang airbase.

March 24 Antiwar teach-in is held at the University of Michigan, Ann Arbor, Michigan. Teach-ins take place throughout 1965 on many college and university campuses.

April North Vietnamese prepare the first launching pad for Russian surface-to-air (SAM) missiles.

May 15 National antiwar teach-in held in Washington, D.C.

May 24 First U.S. Army division leaves U.S. for Vietnam.

June 11 Air Force General Nguyen Cao Ky takes over as South Vietnam's prime minister.

July 28 General William Westmoreland, commander of American forces in Vietnam, asks for and gets an increase in U.S. troops.

October through mid-November U.S. Army soldiers defeat North Vietnamese Army (NVA) troops in the first major battle between American and North Vietnamese forces. The fighting takes place in the remote Ia Drang valley.

December 25 U.S. bombing of North Vietnam is suspended by President Lyndon B. Johnson, who hopes the North Vietnamese will meet with him to talk peace.

December 31 U.S. troop strength in Vietnam numbers 200,000.

1966

January 31 President Johnson orders the bombing of North Vietnam to resume.

January-February The Senate Foreign Relations Committee questions President Johnson's advisers about U.S. involvement in the war.

February 8 President Johnson and South Vietnamese leaders call for peace following a meeting in Hawaii.

March 10 Buddhists demonstrate against the South Vietnamese government. Ky responds by using troops to quell demonstrations.

April 12 B-52 bombers are used for the first time in bombing raids against North Vietnam.

December North Vietnamese leaders meet and agree to fight the war with both troops and diplomacy.

1967

January North Vietnam says that the U.S. must stop its air raids before peace talks can begin.

January Operation Cedar Falls begins. This massive military action is designed to rid the Iron Triangle near Saigon of enemy soldiers. Villages believed sympathetic to the Viet Cong are leveled and the people relocated to refugee camps.

February 22 Operation Junction City begins. A plan to trap Viet Cong in a jungle area northwest of Saigon, the operation results in few VC captured despite five major battles.

April 28 General William Westmoreland addresses Congress on the war in Vietnam, asking for greater support.

July The North Vietnamese meet to plan a "Great Uprising" in 1968 in the south. The uprising became known as the Tet Offensive.

August Secretary of Defense Robert McNamara meets behind closed doors with U.S. senators. He informs them the saturation bombing of North Vietnam is not weakening the North Vietnamese.

September 3 General Nguyen Van Thieu is elected president of South Vietnam.

November U.S. Marines occupy Khe Sanh, a hilltop near the border of Laos. They are soon surrounded by over 35,000 NVA soldiers.

December 31 The number of U.S. troops in Vietnam reaches nearly 500,000.

1968

January 30-31 The Tet Offensive begins as Viet Cong and North Vietnamese troops attack most of the major cities in South Vietnam and the major American military bases.

February 24 U.S. and South Vietnamese forces, after weeks of fighting, retake Hué, ending the Tet Offensive.

March 10 *The New York Times* reports that General William Westmoreland wants 206,000 more American troops by the end of the year.

March 12 Eugene McCarthy, the antiwar U.S. senator from Minnesota, receives 40 percent of the Democratic vote in the New Hampshire primary.

March 16 Between 200 and 600 Vietnamese civilians are murdered by American troops in a village called My Lai 4.

March 31 President Lyndon B. Johnson orders a halt to the bombing of North Vietnam and announces that he will not run again for the presidency.

April 4 Dr. Martin Luther King, Jr., is shot to death in Memphis, Tennessee. Rioting erupts in many large U.S. cities.

May 11 Formal peace talks begin in Paris between the United States and North Vietnam.

June 6 U.S. Senator Robert Kennedy dies the day after he is shot in Los Angeles, California. Kennedy had been campaigning for the Democratic presidential nomination.

June 10 General Creighton Abrams takes command of U.S. forces in Vietnam.

June 27 American troops leave Khe Sanh after several months of bitter fighting.

July 1 U.S. planes resume bombing north of the DMZ.

August 8 Richard M. Nixon is nominated by Republicans to run for the presidency.

August 26-29 Vice President Hubert Humphrey is nominated for the presidency in Chicago as police and antiwar demonstrators clash violently in the city's streets.

November 6 Richard M. Nixon is elected President.

December 31 A total of 540,000 Americans are in Vietnam.

1969

March 18 The secret bombing of Cambodia begins.

March 28 U.S. and ARVN troops discover mass graves of civilians killed by Viet Cong and NVA during the Tet takeover of Hué.

June 8 President Nixon announces that 25,000 American troops will be withdrawn, to be replaced by South Vietnamese forces.

September 3 Ho Chi Minh dies in Hanoi at the age of 79.

Fall Huge antiwar rallies take place in Washington, D.C.

November 16 The country learns of the My Lai 4 massacre.

December 31 The number of U.S. troops in South Vietnam drops to 480,000.

1970

February 20 Henry Kissinger and Le Duc Tho of North Vietnam meet secretly in Paris.

March 18 Prince Sihanouk of Cambodia is overthrown.

April 30 American and South Vietnamese forces invade Cambodia.

May 4 National Guardsmen kill 4 antiwar students and wound 11 others at Kent State University in Ohio.

December 31 The number of U.S. troops in Vietnam falls to 280,000.

1971

January 6 Congress repeals the Gulf of Tonkin Resolution.

February 8 South Vietnamese forces enter Laos in an attempt to cut the Ho Chi Minh trail.

March 29 Lieutenant William Calley is convicted of murder in connection with the massacre at My Lai 4.

December 31 U.S. forces now total 140,000.

1972

May 8 President Nixon orders the mining of Haiphong harbor and steps up the bombing.

June 17 A night watchman catches five men attempting to break into the Democratic national headquarters at the Watergate apartment-hotel complex in Washington, D.C.

November 7 Richard Nixon is re-elected President.

December 31 U.S. combat troops number fewer than 30,000.

1973

January 27 An agreement is reached between the United States and North Vietnam to end the war in South Vietnam.

March 29 The last U.S. troops leave South Vietnam. The only Americans left behind are 8,500 civilians, plus embassy guards and a small number of soldiers in a defense office.

April 5 The U.S. Senate votes 88-3 to forbid aid to Vietnam without congressional approval.

August 15 The bombing of Cambodia by American planes ends. President Nixon criticizes Congress for ending the air war.

October 16 Henry Kissinger and Le Duc Tho are awarded the Nobel Peace Prize for ending the war in Indochina. Tho turns down the award because, as he points out, fighting continues.

1974

April 4 The U.S. House of Representatives rejects a White House proposal for more aid to South Vietnam.

August 9 Richard M. Nixon resigns as President of the United States and thus stops impeachment proceedings. Vice President Gerald Ford is sworn in as President.

1975

January 6 The province of Phuoc Long, only 60 miles north of Saigon, is captured by the communists.

March 14 President Nguyen Van Thieu decides to pull his troops out of the central highlands and northern provinces.

April 8 A huge U.S. cargo plane, loaded with Vietnamese orphans, crashes on takeoff near Saigon. More than 100 children die.

April 17 Cambodia falls to the Khmer Rouge (Cambodian communists).

April 30 Saigon falls to the Vietnamese communists.

December 3 Laos falls to the Pathet Lao (Laotian communists).

1976

July 2 The two Vietnams are officially reunified.

November 2 James Earl (Jimmy) Carter is elected President of the United States.

1977

January 21 President Carter pardons 10,000 draft evaders. Throughout the year more and more refugees ("boat people") leave Vietnam by any means available. Many are ethnic Chinese who fear persecution from Vietnamese victors.

1978

December Vietnamese forces occupy Cambodia.

1979

February 17 China invades Vietnam and is in the country for three weeks.

November 24 The U.S General Accounting Office indicates that thousands of Vietnam veterans were exposed to the herbicide known as Agent Orange. The veterans claim they have suffered physical and psychological damage from the exposure.

1980

Summer Vietnamese army pursues Cambodians into Thailand.

November 4 Ronald Reagan is
elected President of the United
States.

1982

November 13 The Vietnam
Veterans' Memorial is
dedicated in Washington, D.C.

1984

May 7 Seven U.S. chemical
companies agree to an out-of-
court settlement with Vietnam
veterans over manufacture of
the herbicide Agent Orange.
The settlement is for $180
million.

July 15 Major fighting breaks out
along the Vietnam-China
border.

1986

December Vietnam's aging
leaders step down after failing
to improve the economy.

1988

June Vietnamese troops begin to
withdraw from Cambodia.

Emperor Bao Dai.

Glossary

The glossary of each book in this series introduces various Vietnamese and American terms used throughout the war.

Ao dai (pronounced *ow die*): A tunic with long, flowing panels worn over loose-fitting pants. This is the national attire of middle-class Vietnamese women.

Armored personnel carrier (APC): These armor-plated boxes on treads carry eight to ten infantrymen into battle. A driver sits in front and a commander on top of the APCs. The vehicles carry a machine gun but can be penetrated by a large-caliber machine gun bullet or upended by running over a mine.

Army of the Republic of Vietnam (ARVN): The South Vietnamese army, made up largely of draftees.

Binh Xuyen (pronounced *bin zwen*): A gang of about 40,000 men who ran the drug and other crime rings in Saigon when Diem came to power in 1955. The Binh Xuyen was defeated by Diem forces. Many members then joined the Viet Cong.

Bonze: A Buddhist priest.

Buddhism: One of the world's great religions, Buddhism began in northern India and spread to China and Southeast Asia. It teaches that right thinking and self-denial will free the soul from all pain and sorrow. Buddhism was founded by Siddhartha Gautama (Buddha). Most Vietnamese are Buddhists.

Capitalism: An economic system in which the means of production and distribution are privately owned and operated for profit.

Cao Dai (pronounced *cow die*): A religious sect begun in Vietnam in 1925. It recognizes all the world's religions and has many saints from Joan of Arc to Charlie Chaplin. By 1954, there were about 20,000 Cao Dai followers in South Vietnam.

Central Intelligence Agency (CIA): An official American intelligence agency. This group gathers information on friend and foe alike for officials in Washington, D.C. CIA agents operated in Vietnam from before the end of World War II. They did everything from run their own airline to sabotage North Vietnamese industry.

Communism: An economic system that seeks to end private

ownership. All land and other means of production and distribution are owned by the state, which is defined as all the citizens.

Confucianism: A philosophy, based on ancestor worship, that established rules of good government and right conduct to achieve a true way of life. Founded in China by Confucius, a teacher who looked for answers in the past, this philosophy greatly influences many Vietnamese.

Counterinsurgency: Techniques devised to prevent people from rising up against the government. The techniques can range from domestic programs to propaganda to military operations. Americans used many counterinsurgency techniques.

Democracy: Government by the people, either through direct participation of the citizens or through their elected representatives.

Democratic Republic of Vietnam: North Vietnam.

Escalation: The planned, step-by-step increase in intensity of an activity such as war. In the Vietnam conflict, for example, the U.S. escalated the war by increasing the number of combat troops and bombing raids.

Green Berets: U.S. Special Forces soldiers trained in guerrilla warfare. These men taught Vietnamese and Montagnards self-defense and antiguerrilla tactics.

Guerrillas: Civilian soldiers who operate in small groups and make surprise raids on government forces and property. The Viet Cong were considered guerrilla fighters.

Hoa Hao (pronounced *wha ho*): A religious sect founded in 1939 that was a kind of reformed Buddhism. It gained popularity in the Mekong Delta and was anti-French and democratic.

Ho Chi Minh Trail: The path taken by infiltrating North Vietnamese soldiers and civilians bringing weapons and supplies to the Viet Cong. The trail, which was a highway in places, began in North Vietnam and went through parts of Laos and Cambodia.

Indochina: A word conceived by the French for Southeast Asia. The word means "the land between India and China." French Indochina consisted of Laos, Cambodia, and the three French states of Vietnam: Tonkin, Annam, and Cochin China.

Infiltration: As used by Americans, infiltration meant the gradual entry into South Vietnam of northern communist forces. Many came down the Ho Chi Minh Trail.

Mandarins: Vietnamese trained as government officials. These people are at the top of Confucian society and are expected to govern well.

Mekong Delta: Rich floodplain in the extreme south of Vietnam where most rice is grown. The area was created by the Mekong River and was the site of constant guerrilla activity.

Military Assistance Command, Vietnam (MACV): Located in Saigon, MACV was the command headquarters for all U.S. forces in Vietnam.

Montagnards (pronounced *Moan tan yards*): Primitive tribes living in Vietnam's highlands and in other mountainous areas of Southeast Asia. A total of 700,000 were in Vietnam in 1954. They fought alongside U.S. forces and were one of our strongest allies in the war.

Napalm: Jellied fuel packed in bombs that exploded on impact. It was also used in flamethrowers. It showered an area with sticky, flowing fire that caused severe burns which took months to heal. Napalm was introduced in Vietnam by the French and used extensively by the U.S.

National Liberation Front (NLF): Formed in 1960, the NLF represented communist and other political organizations that wanted a reunified Vietnam. As the communists eased others out or absorbed them, the NLF began to answer only to the North Vietnamese. The military arm of this group was the Viet Cong.

Nguyen (pronounced *Nwen*): The most common family name in Vietnam. Half of all Vietnamese are named Nguyen.

Nuoc mam (pronounced *nook mom*): A fermented fish sauce eaten by the Vietnamese. This sauce smells bad but tastes good and accompanies rice, meat, or vegetables at a meal.

People's Army of Vietnam (PAVN): This was the official name and abbreviation for the army of the Democratic Republic of Vietnam (North Vietnam). It was later referred to as the North Vietnamese Army (NVA).

Personalism: The philosophy of the Ngo family, who ruled South Vietnam from 1954 to 1963. Supposedly the opposite of communism, personalism was never really defined by President Diem or Nhu, who was Diem's brother and chief adviser.

Red River Delta: A floodplain created by the Red River east of Hanoi in North Vietnam. Although not as fertile or as large as the Mekong Delta, this area is still heavily populated.

Sabotage: Destruction of roads, bridges, machines and equipment, and other strategic targets by enemy agents.

Self-determination: The principle of allowing a country to decide what kind of government and society it wants, usually determined by free elections.

Strategic hamlets: Villages that were fortified and considered safe from Viet Cong attack. Vietnamese peasants were moved into such villages, often against their will. Many of these hamlets were far from the land the peasants farmed.

Tet: Chinese and Vietnamese new year celebration. Based on the lunar calendar, it occurs in late January or early February.

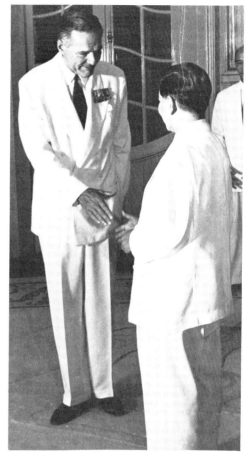

U.S. Ambassador Henry Cabot Lodge towers over Vietnam President Ngo Dinh Diem.

Viet Cong: Guerrilla forces fighting against the South Vietnamese government and against U.S. troops and advisers.

Viet Minh: Guerrilla forces fighting the Japanese and the French. The Viet Minh later became the North Vietnamese Army.

Index

Free Speech Movement, 112, 114
French Foreign Legion, 34
French Indochina Union, 16
Fulbright, William, 104

G

Giap. *See Vo Nguyen Giap*
Goldwater, Barry, 86
Green Berets, 69-70, 101
Gulf of Tonkin incident, 102-104
Gulf of Tonkin Resolution, 104

H

Haiphong, 36, 121
Hanoi, 25, 36, 121
Hmong tribespeople, 70
Ho Chi Minh, 18, 20-21, 25, 29, 30, 31-32, 36, 62, 99, 123
biography of, 18
Ho Chi Minh Trail, 70, 97, 99, 101, 108

I

Indochinese Communist Party, 20
Indonesia, 66, 121
Integration, 60, 62

J

Japanese, 20-21, 23, 25, 27, 29
Johnson, Lyndon B., 68, 84, 86, 100-101, 108, 110

biography of, 100-101
and Gulf of Tonkin incident, 103-104

K

Kennedy, John F., 68, 69, 75, 84, 86
biography of, 83
Kennedy, Robert F., 75
Korea, 48, 121

L

Language, Vietnamese, 16, 51
Laos, 25, 66, 101
and French Indochina Union, 16
secret operations in, 70, 79
Lodge, Henry Cabot, 76
biography of, 76

M

Madame Ngo Dinh Nhu, 65-66, 78-79, 83, 86
biography of, 66
Maddox, 102-103
Malaysia, 66
Mao Zedong, 21
Marines, U. S., 118-119, 121, 123
McGovern, James, 48
McNamara, Robert F., 75, 90, 97
Mekong Delta, 14, 97
Mekong River, 14
Mines, 92, 94
Montagnards, 56, 70, 101

Index

aid to South Vietnam, 66,
68-70, 73
and domino theory, 34
and Indochina, 21, 23
and integration, 60, 62
after Korean War, 60, 62
and policy of containment,
33-34
United States military
advisers, 68-70, 90, 92, 99
Marines, 118-119, 123
pilots, 21, 23, 105, 117
prisoners of war, 105
See also Green Berets
**U.S. Agency for
International
Development** (USAID),
104-105

V

Viet Cong, 88, 90, 92, 94, 97,
100, 101, 108, 117, 121
and strategic hamlet
program, 77
terrorist tactics of, 67-68, 71, 73
Viet Minh, 21, 30, 38, 40-41,
46-48
Vietnam
under Chinese, 14
climate of, 55-56
division into North and
South, 62
drug trade in, 29-31
economy of, 54-55
education in, 57-58
and European invasion, 14, 15
and First Indochina War, 36-48
and French Indochina
Union, 16

under French rule, 14, 16-
18, 20-21, 23, 25, 27
independence of, 29
under Japanese rule, 27, 29
religion in, 56-57
terrain of, 56
*See also North Vietnam;
South Vietnam*
Vietnamese
clothing of, 52
early people, 14
family life of, 58, 88-89
food of, 51-52
under French rule, 25, 27
homes of, 52, 54
under Japanese rule, 27, 29
language, 16, 51
marriage of, 58, 88-89
names of, 57
secret organizations of, 17- 18
Vietnam War
antiwar movement, 112, 114
and draft, 114-115, 117
first combat troops sent,
118-119
and Gulf of Tonkin
incident, 102-104
and Johnson years, 86,
101-110, 114-123
questions about, 12, 14
Vinh-Yen, 42
Vo Nguyen Giap, 30, 40, 42
biography of, 30

W-Y

Westmoreland, William, 108
Women, 88-89
World War II, 20-21, 23, 30, 32
Yen Do, 62, 64

A U.S. Marine armored personnel carrier takes South Vietnamese troops across a canal in an area 50 miles south of Saigon.

Acknowledgments

The series *War in Vietnam* is the product of many talented and dedicated people. Their stories, experiences, and skills helped make this series a unique contribution to our knowledge of the Vietnam era.

Author David K. Wright would like to thank the following people for their assistance: Yen Do, former Saigon resident and now a newspaper publisher in California; David Doyle, who works with resettled Hmong people from Laos; John Kuehl and Don Luce, both employees of Asia Resource Center in Washington, D. C.; Patricia (Kit) Norland of the Indochina Project in Washington, D. C.; John Stolting, 9th Infantry Division, Awards and Decorations section; and Frank Tatu, Don Ehlke, and Donald Wright, all veterans of the Vietnam War. These individuals gave generously of their time in personal interviews and provided resources on Southeast Asian history and current conditions.

A special thanks to Frank Burdick, Professor of History at State University College in Cortland, New York. Professor Burdick reviewed the manuscripts and made many valuable suggestions to improve them.

The editorial staff at Childrens Press who produced the four books of this series include Fran Dyra, Vice President, Editorial; Margrit Fiddle, Creative Director; L. Sue Baugh, Project Editor; Judy Feldman, Photo Editor; and Pat Stahl and Norman Zuefle, Editorial Proofreaders. Charles Hills of New Horizons & Associates created the dramatic book design for the series.

Picture Acknowledgments

The Bettmann Archive—9, 19, 21, 31, 32, 33, 39, 45, 49-both images, 50, 53, 54, 61, 71, 96-97, 120, 131

Black Star:

© Andrew Rakoczy—Front Cover

© Lee Lockwood—2-3, 34-35

© Matt Franjola—22-23

© Bob Klein—57

© Gene Daniels—87

© Robert Ellison—88

Wide World Photos, Inc.—4, 5, 8, 10-11, 13, 17, 18, 20, 24, 26, 28, 30, 37, 40-41, 42, 43, 47, 48-49, 55, 58-59, 63, 64, 65, 66, 67, 68, 69, 72-73, 74, 76, 78-79, 80-81, 82, 83, 84-85, 89-both images, 91, 92-93, 94-95, 98, 100, 103, 105, 106-107, 108, 109, 111, 113, 114, 115, 116, 118, 119, 122-123, 135, 140-141, Back Cover

Maps—15, 16, 44, 102, 104

About the Author

David K. Wright is a freelance writer who lives in Wisconsin. He grew up in and around Richmond, Indiana, and graduated from Wittenberg University in Springfield, Ohio, in 1966.

Wright received his draft notice the day after he graduated from college. He was inducted in September 1966 and arrived in Vietnam at Bien Hoa in March 1967. He served in the U.S. Army 9th Infantry Division as an armor crewman. Wright was stationed at Camp Bearcat, east of Saigon, and at Dong Tam in the Mekong Delta. He returned from Vietnam in March 1968 and was honorably discharged in September of that year, having attained the rank of Specialist five.

This is the first in a series of four books by Wright for Childrens Press about the Vietnam War. He also has written a book on Vietnam and a book on Malaysia in the *Enchantment of the World* series also published by Childrens Press.